FREDDY SHEPHERD
CHAIRMAN, NEWCASTLE UNITED

ALAN SHEARER

A legend
IN THE
FOOTBALL WORLD

There are players, there are great players, and there are legends, and Alan Shearer is without doubt a footballing legend.

In 10 magnificent years at Newcastle United, Alan has become one of the great Tyneside heroes of all time, and has more than justified the world record fee we paid to bring him here from Blackburn Rovers in July 1996.

Records stand proudly in posterity, and Alan Shearer has established many in his time, but what Alan has achieved takes him far beyond mere records. He has become a symbol of Tyneside and an iconic figure for every Geordie as well as an internationally-respected figure.

Now, tonight, as Alan takes his thoroughly-deserved testimonial at a packed St. James' Park, we are paying tribute to a man who has raised the profile of Newcastle United Football Club to a new level and written a special chapter in the club's history.

When Alan came here in 1996, he was already established as one of the world's leading strikers. There were many competitors for his signature, but as a true Geordie he chose to come home to Newcastle United.

His loyalty to the club has never wavered, and our supporters' faith in him has been strong, constant, and amply rewarded.

Tonight, that faith will be seen in the unique and conclusive context of a testimonial match and undoubtedly the emotional send-off the Geordie Nation affords one of its own here this evening will be sincere and heartfelt.

It is fitting that, on such an occasion, one of Britain's finest clubs, the Scottish champions Glasgow Celtic, will provide the opposition.

On behalf of everyone at Newcastle United, and on behalf of Alan Shearer in particular, I warmly welcome the directors, officials, players and supporters of Celtic to St. James' Park and thank them for their contribution to what will be one of the most memorable nights ever seen here.

In his generosity, Alan has chosen to donate all proceeds from this evening's match to his chosen charities – a gesture typical of the man, and one which means every paying spectator here this evening has made his or her contribution to very worthy causes.

Of course, there is no cause more worthy than Alan Shearer himself, and as he takes his final bows on the pitch tonight before retiring as a player, Geordieland will embrace one of its finest representatives.

Thank you, Alan Shearer, for all you have given us in the last decade.

I am sure football will still have a place for you in the future, and wherever your path leads, we wish you and your family every success and happiness in the years to come.

Alan Shearer Testimonial 2006

TESTIMONIAL NIGHT SCHEDULE (PLEASE LISTEN CLOSELY TO PA ANNOUNCEMENTS THROUGHOUT THE EVENING)

5pm	TURNSTILES OPEN
5pm	PLAYERS WARM-UP
5pm	**KEEDIE** PERFORMS 'NESSUN DORMA' We would request supporters to be in their seats at this time.

0pm	TEAMS ENTER THE PITCH

When Alan emerges from the tunnel if you are sitting in the North, ... and East Stands - please hold your seat card above your head with the ... side facing towards the pitch to create a spectacular effect...

7.45pm	KICK-OFF
8.30pm	HALF-TIME PENALTY COMPETITION **England v Scotland**
8.45pm	SECOND HALF
9.30 pm	FULL-TIME

■ Following the final whistle there will be an interview with United's record goalscorer and a number of presentations all hosted by **ANT & DEC**

WE WOULD ASK ALL SUPPORTERS TO REMAIN SEATED UNTIL AFTER THE PRESENTATIONS HAVE FINISHED AND ALAN HAS LEFT THE PITCH FOR THE FINAL TIME. ENJOY YOUR EVENING

Alan Shearer Testimonial 2006

ALAN SHEARER tonight says farewell to football as a player after 10 years with Newcastle United and 18 years in the game.

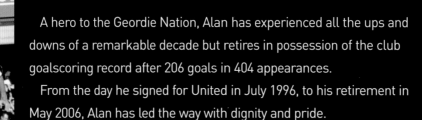

A hero to the Geordie Nation, Alan has experienced all the ups and downs of a remarkable decade but retires in possession of the club goalscoring record after 206 goals in 404 appearances.

From the day he signed for United in July 1996, to his retirement in May 2006, Alan has led the way with dignity and pride.

Now he looks back over a dramatic decade at St. James' Park ...

By 1996, Alan Shearer was already a world-famous figure. A Championship winner with Blackburn Rovers after four formative years at Southampton, he was much in demand when the big names came calling ten summers ago. And his options presented him with a dilemma that would eventually be resolved by his own Geordie heart.

I HAD FOUR CHOICES...

One was to stay at Blackburn. I also had the choice to go to Newcastle, to go to Manchester United, or to go to Liverpool.

It was a massive decision for me and when I flew over to Jack (Walker, the Blackburn owner) – Jack put his jet on to fly me to Jersey – I spent the afternoon there and had made my mind up to stay at Blackburn. I listened to what he had to say, and I thought I would come home to think on it and discuss it with the family, as you do.

Blackburn even offered me the manager's job, but at 26 that was ridiculously early.

And then I decided that if I was going to make the right decision, it was fair that I met everyone.

I had met Alex Ferguson, and I had met Kevin Keegan. Freddy Shepherd, Douglas Hall ... I got on great with them. Everyone was great. Everything was fine. I got on with them and liked what I heard. And Newcastle was my home-town club.

I also got on with Alex Ferguson at Manchester United. I had a chat with him and he was fine. I didn't want to go abroad, so it was a matter of deciding which of the English teams I wanted to play for. I've never really fancied going abroad, so I had met all the relevant parties and my mind was everywhere, to be honest.

But one night I suddenly said to Lainya: 'That's it – I'm coming home.' It was the pull of playing for Newcastle – the No 9 shirt and all that. I wrote down the plusses and the negatives on everything. And I defy anyone to tell me that I didn't do the right thing.

It's been everything I wanted it to be. I've lived my dream. I've lived for my boyhood shirt and got the record – and that's a great trophy to have.

We've had some great times and some desperate times. Kevin Keegan left after six months, which was obviously disappointing, but there have been so many good things about playing for Newcastle United since then.

I signed for Newcastle and had my medical in, of all places, Manchester! I passed my medical and they said to me: 'You're going to the Far East – we would like you to come.' I said: 'When?' And they said: 'In about three hours!'

We flew from Manchester, we were living in Formby, so Lainya packed me a bag and put it in a cab, I got my bag at the airport, and I met up with the lads in the Far East. And I never ever went back to that house!

By the time we flew back, we went straight to Newcastle and it was the press conference at St. James'. By then Lainya had had to pack the house up by herself and sell the house herself – which she did. So at least the move got me out of packing the house up! I went to the Gosforth Park Hotel – and I was a Newcastle United player ...

ALAN DIDN'T HAVE THE GREATEST START TO HIS CAREER AT NEWCASTLE. A HEAVY CHARITY SHIELD DEFEAT WAS FOLLOWED BY A FIRST-DAY PREMIER LEAGUE REVERSE AT EVERTON. BUT THEN IT STARTED TO GO RIGHT ...

We had the Charity Shield which was 4-0 to Manchester United. And then we had Everton away and we got beaten 2-0 and I thought: 'Jesus – what have I done here?' I was serious. I thought: 'We've been done by Man U, at Everton I've had a goal disallowed – and I never pushed him – but that was us off to a poor start.'

I had to wait until the Wimbledon goal in the next game on my home debut – after 86 minutes – and it was a brilliant feeling. There was excitement, because I had always wanted to do it. And my parents and family were there.

It would still have been a great night even had I not scored. I had achieved something I had always wanted to do. There were butterflies of excitement. I just wanted to get out there.

There were a lot of special moments after that in that first season here, not least in the 5-0 against Man United in the October.

As the world's most expensive player, it was always nice for anyone going to a new club to score a goal. You are judged on goals, and you have to score them.

Soon after Wimbledon we played my old team Blackburn at home and the one big thing I did think about in the Blackburn game was my old mate Tim Flowers being in goal for them. He knew my game inside out – I'd travelled with him in a car to training all the time. If anyone was going to know me, Tim was going to know me.

Then when we got a penalty against Rovers (and I took them against him day-to-day in practice) he knew what I was thinking. He's a big mate. But I scored – even though Tim went the right way.

I knew what the stadium was like and I knew what the fans were like. I knew what the Newcastle team was like because I had sat and watched them. Les Ferdinand was my best strike partner ever at club level though we only had one season together. He had pace and it was a great combination.

We also had Ginola, Gillespie, Beardsley, Lee ... it was a team designed to score goals and get forward and me and Les were at the front of it. It was a very good team – I knew that. The 5-0 v Man U was a special game, particularly because of what had happened in the Charity Shield, but there were so many special matches.

SHEARER

On Kevin Keegan, I still don't know the reason he left. I really don't. But it was traumatic for everyone. Everyone got on very well with him. We had a great relationship, training was good and the football was going brilliantly. We were going well, and we beat Tottenham 7-1 and Leeds 3-0 just before he left.

I don't know what was going on. On the Monday morning Terry Mac came in and said he had something to tell us. We could hardly believe it when we heard what it was.

We were still going well in the league. I didn't speak to Kevin for a few weeks after that because he left the country. He was one of my heroes when I was a kid and one of the reasons I came to Newcastle. Everyone was fond of him – all the players here loved him and all the fans loved him. He was a hero.

But you can never sign for a club because of the manager. In football the manager can be gone – that's the nature of football. People come and go. You know that when you come into this game.

ALAN'S FORMER MANAGER AT BLACKBURN, KENNY DALGLISH, WAS THE MAN WHO REPLACED KEVIN KEEGAN AT ST. JAMES' PARK IN 1997.

I was delighted when Newcastle chose Kenny Dalglish because he had won the league at Liverpool and Blackburn; at Blackburn when I was playing there, of, course.

We didn't get results because the players weren't good enough – that's the simple reason. If you go round every player, they just weren't good enough.

Kenny was an unbelievable player, and a great manager. He never criticised anyone in public. I still to this day think Kenny was brilliant as a manager.

But Les Ferdinand leaving in the pre-season of 1997 just when I got the bad injury at Everton was a loss. The club had agreed a deal and then when I got injured they tried to get Les back. But Les had been told he was leaving, or that they were selling him. And from that point Kenny was in a no-win situation. He was left with Jon Dahl Tomasson, Tino, and John Barnes and Rushie came in. Temuri also was there.

Jon Dahl Tomasson has gone on to play for AC Milan and win the Champions League - he was a good player, but the right player at the wrong time. If he had scored one of those two one-on-ones against Sheffield Wednesday in his first game for us it would have been a different Jon Dahl. But he had to play a different role to what he was accustomed to and it didn't work for him. So that made it extremely difficult.

The injury made it a tough time. It was probably my worst injury, if I'm honest. I remember lying in the hospital bed and the radiographer saying: 'I've got some good news and some bad news.'

He said the good news is that you are still alive – the person who was in this bed before you isn't. The bad news is that you have ruptured the ligaments, chipped the bone ... etc etc ... it didn't help me when my ankle was pointing in the wrong direction and they had to straighten it without anaesthetic. I had to have gas and air. The pain was horrendous.

The surgeon, Rob Gregory, was due to go on holiday but stayed behind to come and do the op. I think you always believe you will come back - it was just a matter of when – but the question is: will you come back the same?

I never doubted I would. I always believed, and was confident, I would. I had done it at the end of July and I came back in the January in a match against Bolton which stands out in my mind because of Temuri Ketsbaia, who went mad at the end after scoring the winner in the last minute.

It had been tedious hard work getting back from such a long-term injury, so it was just pleasing to get back out on the pitch again. Scoring at Stevenage in the FA Cup after three minutes following that was a great way back, and my goals against Stevenage – I also got two in the replay at St. James' Park – were important to me.

For the first three, four, five games you are playing on adrenaline – you run around sometimes like a headless chicken. It's only after those first few games that you realise you're not really match-fit.

And I missed out on the Champions League, the Barcelona game and all the others. I had worked so hard in the previous season to get us there and missing out on the Champions League was the down-side.

I've suffered more than most with injuries and but for the three serious injuries I would have had a lot more goals. But I guess I haven't done badly.

THE OLD TRAFFORD FA CUP SEMI-FINALS OF 1998 AND 1999, WHEN ALAN SCORED IN THE 1-0 VICTORY OVER SHEFFIELD UNITED AND BOTH GOALS IN THE 2-0 VICTORY OVER TOTTENHAM HOTSPUR, WERE CAREER PEAKS AT UNITED. BUT THERE WERE ALSO MAJOR DISAPPOINTMENTS

We had the semi-finals at Old Trafford against Sheffield United and Tottenham. The semis were great, but the Finals were bitterly disappointing – it was just our luck that when we got to the Finals we got teams going for the Double and Treble.

We didn't perform in either Cup Final. We hit the bar –

Nikos – in the '98 Final again
the post – and Temuri hit the
against Manchester United,
winning. If we'd played bette
different.

But the biggest disappoin
Sporting Lisbon defeat last
was the biggest let-down in
disappointment of losing in
best chance we had of winr
here. And particularly after
two goals ahead on aggreg
that were left in it ...

It was as shattering as th
Kieron and we were better

We lost 4-1 and then we
the FA Cup semi-final at C
Sunday, and we were with
didn't come out with any c
don't perform you don't w

SHEARER

THEN THINGS BECAME REALLY DIFFICULT AT THE END OF RUUD GULLIT'S YEAR IN CHARGE. EVERY NEWCASTLE FAN REMEMBERS THE SIGHT OF ALAN AND DUNCAN FERGUSON SITTING IN THE ST. JAMES' PARK DUG-OUT FOR THE DERBY DEFEAT AGAINST SUNDERLAND IN THE POURING RAIN

I never had a problem with Ruud Gullit at first, and if anyone said to me then that I did have a problem I'd have told them I didn't.

But I don't think it was a coincidence that Stuart Pearce was left out, John Barnes was left out, Rob Lee was left out ... they are all big names. It wasn't coincidence that they were all shoved to one side. And that wasn't nice.

Yet every manager is entitled to do the job in whatever way he feels is correct. He has the opportunity to play whatever game with whatever players he wishes. You have to go along with it and he chose to leave me out of the Sunderland game.

But it was particularly disappointing to be left out – and disappointing also to only find out from the notice board shortly before the game when the teamsheet went up.

Looking back now, you can laugh. But it wasn't funny at the time. Me and Big Dunc were left out. When Dunc went on it was 1-0 to us and when I went on it was 1-1, Sunderland scored after each substitution, and Gullit pointed out afterwards that our coming on had preceded goals for Sunderland.

The door was already hanging off the manager's office at the training ground the next morning when I got there. Big Dunc had beaten me to it. Let's just say I expressed my disappointment, and so did Dunc.

If Ruud Gullit hadn't left and if the situation hadn't changed, I would have had to leave Newcastle United, because it would have been quite clear that I wasn't the flavour of the month, which is fine in its way because not everyone in this world gets on. But I would have had to leave – and I would have left.

HOWEVER, GULLIT RESIGNED AND NORTH-EASTERNER BOBBY ROBSON REPLACED HIM IN THE AUTUMN OF 1999. AND ALAN REMAINED A NEWCASTLE UNITED PLAYER

Bobby Robson coming in was great because he was a world-renowned manager who was desperate to come to Newcastle and do well.

We had lost that quality side. We were heading towards the Second Division. It wasn't a great club at that time because results weren't going for us. We needed a bit of direction and Bobby got everyone playing with smiles on their faces again. He got everybody back together, and the results improved. His first home game was the 8-0 win against Sheffield Wednesday, when I scored five.

With me, Bobby said he could only see the front of me rather than the back of me because I was receiving everything with my back to goal, and he got me turning to beat the defenders. And I reaped the benefit.

We should have got a result at Chelsea in his first game, when we lost 1-0, and then the 8-0 against Sheff Wed was a great day. It just gave everyone self-belief again. We got it up and going again and got a lot of decent results.

Once Bobby had had a chat with me and five or six other lads, and explained what he wanted to do and what he was going to do, he got everybody going again and raised the morale of the club.

There WAS a lot of unrest, and he did a great job in settling that. If you have a happy football club, you have got a chance. You can't keep everybody happy all the time, but there's a way of keeping people generally happy and Bobby Robson did that.

Within two years we went from second-bottom to third – and that's an achievement. I finally got the Champions League I'd missed in 1997-98. I'd played in the Champions League for Blackburn in 1995-96 but we didn't do well and in 2002-03 Newcastle did do well. We became the first team ever to qualify for the second stage after losing its first three first stage group games. And we were climbing the table and getting to third and fourth.

Craig Bellamy was my front partner and it was a pace-and-power partnership with him. His pace was great and meant we could get in behind teams.

That team was not far behind the '97 team when you look at it, and look at the league positions. But it never quite reached the peaks of the '96 team.

One of the great disappointments, though, was the defeat by Partizan Belgrade in the Champions League qualifier in 2003-04.

Nobby had scored when we'd won 1-0 out in Belgrade, but we blew it in the return at St. James', went down 1-0 and lost on penalties. That was certainly a real downer, and it took us a long time to get over it, and it took the fans a long time to get over it. But we did quite well in the league that season.

ALAN WAS ORIGINALLY PLANNING TO RETIRE FROM PLAYING IN 2005. BUT HE DECIDED TO PLAY ON FOR ANOTHER YEAR

I was going to retire last year but at the time things were going great, we were on a run, and I felt I was playing well and scoring goals. I spoke to everyone and everyone was telling me I should carry on.

I always promised myself I would finish at the top, and things were going that well and I was feeling physically so good that I felt I would still be at the top in another year.

We had a great trip to Dubai, we came back, and I signed the contract on April 1st. On April 2nd we played Aston Villa at home and bang – that was it. It was a nightmare of an afternoon. We lost 3-0, had three players sent off, and it all went wrong from there. Lee Bowyer got suspended for a long time and we just went from bad to worse.

We had been all going along quite nicely – the quarter-final of the UEFA Cup and the semi-final of the FA Cup – but it's amazing what can, and did, happen in such a short space of time. Just when you think you've cracked it, it all goes wrong.

There was never any thought in my mind when I decided to play on of breaking the club scoring record – because never did I think I was going to do that. I was going to retire, then I wasn't going to play a full season, instead just play a small part to help the club.

But we got a lot of injuries this season – Michael Owen in particular – and I had to play regularly. I didn't expect to play all these games, and it has been physically tough for me.

I've only played seven or eight times with Michael and that's a shame because our record together in those games has been very good. When we've played together, Michael's scored and I've scored. I wish we could have played together more often.

SHEARE

QUIT INTERNATIONAL FOOTBALL. AND HE HAS NEVER REGRETTED THAT DECISION.

When I retired from the international scene, it was the travelling, not so much the games, that I wanted to get away from.

It was a hard slog at international level. I had the serious injuries and something would have caught up with me – I'm pretty sure of that. And ultimately Newcastle United would have suffered.

I was hardly seeing anything of my family. We had another child on the

caught up with me. What's more, I would have been finished playing football earlier than this if I had been still playing for England.

So I have no regrets. I know when the time is right to step away.

In 2005-06 there have been times when I've felt tired and struggled. I'm the first to admit this is a different Alan Shearer to a few years ago. One – I've got less hair. Two – I'm not as quick. Three – I'm not scoring as many goals. It's not the Alan Shearer of 1996, or even 2000.

By the same token, you will see a different Michael Owen, a different Ronaldo, in 10 years' time. But I still

I really do.

At the end, there was a bit of sadness. Getting injured at Sunderland took away my last three games for Newcastle, but scoring and winning 4-1 at Sunderland wasn't a bad way to go out, was it.

Whatever, though, I've been a very lucky lad. I've lived my dream, I've played centre-forward for Newcastle United, I've got the club's goalscoring record.

And I've played for the Geordie fans, which is one of the greatest things anyone can ever do.

"I'VE PLAYED FOR THE GEORDIE FANS, WHICH IS ONE OF THE GREATEST THINGS ANYONE CAN EVER DO"

SO WHAT DOES THE FUTURE HOLD?

Now I'm going to have some quality time with my family, which is something I've never had over the last 18 years and more. I'm not complaining, because it's been a fabulous time, but a footballer's life isn't the best for family life.

I'm going to do some media work for however long. I'm doing the World Cup in Germany for the BBC this summer. You may see me the odd Saturday night on Match of the Day.

But you will also see me having a nice family Christmas and New Year, and nice family holidays.

I've had people telling me where to be and what to do next ever since I left school at 15. So I'm looking forward to the freedom. I will enjoy that.

But I'm taking my coaching badges and I would like to give management a go one day. However, as with everything, that will be when I feel the time is right. If the time was right, and I felt right to go into it, then I'll do it one day.

I love golf and horse-racing. There are no phones out on the golf course, and horse-racing is a great day out. I've got a share in horses and there's a buzz in going out and watching them race – and sometimes winning!

And I will be here at St. James' whenever I can, watching my team, Newcastle United. I've got my box and I will be here watching the games at every opportunity.

As the fan I have always been and will always be.

... "SIGN SHEARER AND BRING GOALS TO NEWCASTLE"

At the end of the 1995-96 season, Newcastle United fans could only cast envious glances in the direction of their Manchester United counterparts as the relentless Red Devils chased down Kevin Keegan's Magpies to clinch the Premiership title on the final day of a long and eventful campaign.

That summer, however, Geordie spirits would be soaring again as Newcastle put one over the men from Old Trafford in the race for another huge footballing prize ... the signature of England striker Alan Shearer.

The mission for directors Freddy Shepherd and Douglas Hall was this: Sign Shearer and bring goals to Newcastle.

And here, in their own words, is how they pulled off a stunning signing that made headlines around the world.

"It was the close season in 1996 when we heard that Alan might be available for transfer from Blackburn Rovers.

"We had just been pipped for the title by Manchester United and we knew, of course, that they would be strongly interested in signing Alan as well if he were available.

"We contacted Blackburn Rovers and received permission to speak to Alan and his agent. This came just as we were about to go away on a club tour to the Far East, so we knew time was of the essence.

"At that time we received a telephone call from Martin Edwards at Manchester United who confirmed their interest in the player.

"We both agreed we were not going to go past £10m and then it would be up to Alan to decide which club, if either, he wanted to join.

"If one of the clubs decided to then up their bid they would contact the other, so there was a gentleman's agreement to keep each other informed.

"A meeting was arranged at a farmhouse in the North-West and we both drove down from Newcastle, accompanied by the club's bank manager from Barclays, Alan Hogg.

"On the way down we took a call from Martin Edwards saying Manchester United were going to increase their bid, and that basically all bets were off.

"We accepted that. It's the way football works and it wasn't unexpected to be honest – it's exactly what any club in a race like this would have done.

"We arrived at the farmhouse to meet Alan and his agent. Kevin was already there as he'd arrived earlier to discuss footballing matters with Alan. By the time we arrived, the football side of things had been sorted – that just left us to sort out the financial side of things.

"When we first spoke to Alan he told us he was happy to join Newcastle if we could do the deal with Blackburn.

"We then got Jack Walker on the telephone and he made it crystal clear to us that he wanted £15m and not a penny less from Newcastle – but that if he went to Manchester United then the price would be considerably higher.

"All credit to Jack, he never wavered from the deal. And that was Jack Walker for you – his word was his bond.

"The deal was as good as done, our bank manager made the financial arrangements, and the rest as they say is history ... Alan was signed and then joined the rest of the squad out in the Far East.

"Driving down to the North-West on that day we were determined to do everything in our power to secure Alan's transfer.

"We knew through our spies that Manchester United had spoken to Alan the day before we met him, and we knew we'd have to work quickly to do the deal.

"It was a world record fee that we paid for Alan and news of the deal travelled right across the world. Alan flew out to the Far East to join the players and was mobbed from the first minute he landed.

"It was a lot of money spent, but history will show what a fantastic servant Alan Shearer proved to be for Newcastle United – and what a brilliant bit of business for the club."

Russell Cushing chats with new boy Shearer before the flight to the Far East.

Welcome Home to the One and Only Alan Shearer

He's Inspiration-AL!

April 1st, 1989 ...
The Dell, Southampton. Glenn Roeder, in his last year as a Newcastle United veteran, is up against an untested 18-year-old striker in the Saints forward line.

Roeder little knew then that he would be managing the same player 17 years later at Newcastle United, and sharing a dug-out with a world-famous superstar as he guided the Magpies up the Premiership table.

"That game at The Dell was the first time I came across Alan," Glenn recalls. "And he made a big impression on me. I got sick of this youngster battering into me, pulling my shirts and shorts, and generally being a heck of a nuisance!"

Southampton won 1-0 with a late Neil Ruddock penalty, United were eventually relegated, and the next time the pair met was in the England camp late in 1996 as Glenn Hoddle prepared his side, including Shearer, for a World Cup qualifier against Italy, and Roeder was operating as a coach alongside Hoddle.

"By then Alan was a real personality," Roeder says. "When he came into a room, you knew he had come into a room. Not a lot of people have that special presence, but Alan does and it has got greater as he's got older.

"He has high standards, loyalty, trust, and humility. He comes from the right school. And you are honoured if you

can call him your friend. If you were in a spot of bother, you would want him with you.

"From those early days with Southampton, Alan has gone on to become a world-class striker – and now I believe he is the last of a dead breed. Sir Alex Ferguson said exactly that last month.

"Alan led the line in the old-fashioned way, rarely giving the ball away. He had the quality and the bravery to score goals, and as a captain he has been inspirational in the way Tony Adams was inspirational at Arsenal.

"Some people have the gift of being inspirational either by their actions or their voice. Alan has the gift of being inspirational in both those respects."

Glenn Roeder

KENNY DALGLISH

Kenny Dalglish managed Alan twice during his managerial career, firstly signing him for Blackburn then linking up with him again at St. James' Park. Kenny smashed the British transfer record when he took Alan to Blackburn from Southampton back in 1992. And when the Championship trophy was being paraded around Ewood Park three years later, Kenny knew it was money well spent...

"It was the record transfer at the time, but I didn't think it was that expensive because I knew what we were getting.

"People suggested he came to Blackburn for the money, but that was a load of rubbish. He came to Blackburn because he was more comfortable coming to the club than he would have been moving anywhere else.

"When he came in, we had just been promoted, it was a transitional period for the club, and the lads who had got us up could have been forgiven for looking at this big-money signing coming in and thinking 'here we go'.

"But he settled in straight away, he was great with the lads, and he mucked in with the rest of them.

"Then in his first league game, Alan scored two great goals down at Crystal Palace – and those fans were delighted!

"He made a huge contribution at Blackburn, right up to winning the title. He just scored goals every week, whether he was alongside Mike Newell, or Chris Sutton, or Roy Wegerle.

"Winning the title is a team effort – but it doesn't do you any harm if you've got Alan Shearer in your side.

"When I came to Newcastle and worked with him again, he hadn't changed. He was still banging in goals.

"I remember his hat-trick against Leicester when we came from 3-1 down to win 4-3. That was typical Alan, he never gave up.

"The other goal that stands out was in the semi-final of the 1998 FA Cup when he scored against Sheffield United.

"You saw what that meant to him, celebrating with 30,000 Geordies at Old Trafford.

"The disappointing thing for me at Newcastle was the fact Alan got that bad injury in a pre-season game at Everton.

"He missed the Champions League qualifiers in Zagreb when we got through, and he missed out on the big games.

"Had he been fit, who knows how we would have done. But it was a shame to see the nights like when Barcelona came here and Tino got the hat-trick, and Alan wasn't part of it.

"The Champions League would have been a great stage for him to play on.

"It hasn't surprised me that he has gone on and reached the levels he has. He may not have won many trophies, but he has certainly enjoyed himself along the way.

"I'm certain tonight will be the swansong that he deserves. You don't need to tell me about the fans of either Newcastle or Celtic – and they're guaranteed to give him the send-off that is fitting for a man of his stature."

"HE WAS A ROLE MODEL ... THE ULTIMATE PROFESSIONAL" SAYS SIR BOBBY ROBSON

ALAN SHEARER wasn't in the Newcastle team when Bobby Robson took over the Gallowgate hot seat back in 1999. Two weeks later, Shearer netted five goals against Sheffield Wednesday in an 8-0 win to mark Bobby's first home game. The rest is history...

"When I took over at Newcastle United, I'd never met Alan.

"I knew of him, of course, but I'd never met him before. I'd watched his career closely over the years, and I'd always admired him, but I never actually met him face to face until the day I walked into St. James' Park.

"When I arrived at the club, he wasn't playing. I looked at him, I looked at his game, and he was only 29 at the time. There was no way he was finished, no way.

"I sat down with him and we talked about his game. I didn't think he was

running at the time, I felt he was static and he'd lost a bit of movement.

"He listened to what I had to say, he took it on board – and in my first home game he went out and scored five goals. He had four or five or six years left in him then – he's proved that since then.

"Had he left the club then, it would have been a tragedy.

"He was an ideal captain. He had everything, on and off the field. When I went out and signed young players like JJ and Bellamy and Milner and Bramble, and so on, I used to say to them – 'look at Shearer'.

"He was great in the dressing-room, he used to have his say at half-time. He was a pleasure to have around and I couldn't have asked for a better professional to have as my captain. He was a role model, the ultimate professional.

"He scored so many goals for me in my five years at the club, and there were some corkers amongst them. I remember the goal he got against Chelsea, when he hit a shot on the turn at the Gallowgate End and it flew into the top corner. We won 2-1 that day.

"There was another one at home to Aston Villa. Robert Lee played a diagonal ball over the top, it came to Alan about thigh high, and he placed a volley across the goalkeeper into the net. Class, absolute class.

"I can't speak highly enough of Alan, and I sincerely hope that he goes on to be a success in whatever he chooses to do next.

"I wish him a wonderful evening, he deserves an occasion like this and I hope he enjoys every second of it."

Goalkeeper **SHAY GIVEN** arrived at Newcastle United a year to the month after Alan Shearer, and from the same club, Blackburn Rovers. And while Alan has been banging the goals in at one end, Shay has been keeping them out at the other.

Shay says: "I was at Blackburn with Alan for a couple of years but didn't really play much with him there, because Tim Flowers was ahead of me in the goalkeeping order.

"But it's been a privilege to have played with him so much here at Newcastle.

"His whole performance level and goalscoring record has been phenomenal and when you see him in front of you it's an inspiration.

"He's a legend – he leads the team on and off the pitch. And everyone, even the young lads at this football club, looks at the captain and sees what he has done throughout his career and tries to emulate it."

Adds Shay with a smile: "Al's a golf bandit as well, mind you – he's certainly taken some money off me over the years. In fact, he's so much of a bandit that he should be wearing a balaclava out on the course!

"And people say he's boring in his interviews. Well, if you speak to the players they'll tell you something very different, for Al's always full of beans and likes to have a joke and a laugh."

"We hit it off straight away, and we went on to become good mates.

"I'm honoured to call myself a friend of his, because he has been an unbelievable ambassador for the club and the city.

"And if I hadn't been out there playing alongside him, I'd have been there in the Gallowgate End watching and cheering all those goals.

"I was playing alongside him when he scored his first goal for the club, and I was alongside him when he equalled the record and went on to break it.

LEE CLARK was as excited as the rest of the Geordie Nation when Alan Shearer signed for the Magpies back in the summer of 1996. Lee tells how he and the rest of the squad found out about the world-record breaking swoop.

"He has given all Geordies something to be proud of over the last 10 years.

"He's a different character when he's away from the cameras, and he's always in amongst the pranksters in the dressing-room.

"I remember the Charity Shield game down at Wembley in 1996, it was a red hot day. We all had to wear the nice club suits and shirts for the day.

"Someone, I can't name names, managed to get into the hotel room of Derek Wright, our physio, took his shirt out of the packet, cut the sleeves off it, then folded it up nicely and slid it back into the packet.

"On the day of the game we all took our jackets off because it was that hot, but Derek was the only one with his suit jacket still on.

"He was sweating buckets, but he couldn't take it off because his shirt was ripped to shreds with no sleeves on it.

"Whether that was Alan or not, I wouldn't like to say...

"It hasn't surprised me that this evening's game was sold out as quickly as it was. He could have probably filled the ground four or fives times over.

"I'm sure he will have a fantastic evening, and I'm privileged to be a part of it."

"We were going on the Far East tour, we were all on the plane and just before the doors were closing we saw Kevin get up and get off.

"We were all quizzing each other, but for the manager to do that ahead of an important pre-season trip we knew it must have been the big one – and we were right.

"Kevin eventually linked up with us out in the Far East and said to us that if we didn't realise we were playing for a big club, then we would now because we had just smashed the world transfer record to bring Alan home.

"We got to meet Alan in Singapore on the second leg of the tour. We hoped he would be the final piece of the jigsaw, and the key to us winning trophies.

"As we all know now, that wasn't to happen – but Alan Shearer, even at 15 million quid, was and still is the biggest bargain this football club has ever had when you consider everything he has done for us.

"His signing gave us all a massive boost, and being a fellow-Geordie I knew what he was all about as we'd followed similar routes as kids.

"For me, that gives me a lot of pleasure.

"I remember once we were going out for a bite to eat and there was a knock at the door. My son Jak opened it, and it was Alan who said 'is your dad in?'.

"The next thing I know Jak was running around singing 'Shearer, Shearer'. He was in awe because he's seen this legend on the telly, then all of a sudden he is knocking at his front door!

"The word legend is often used too easily, but Alan Shearer is definitely in that bracket and he will never be forgotten by the people of the club and the city who were fortunate enough to see him play.

My top nine Newcastle games..

Newcastle United 2
Portsmouth 0
Premier League, St. James' Park, February 4th, 2006

"This one is up there for obvious reasons – it was day I broke the club goalscoring record held previously by Jackie Milburn. It was the best feeli after scoring I ever had in all my 206 goals for Newcastle United, and gave me my most pleasure. The ovation from the fans went for ages after the goal and it was someth I'll never ever forget."

Newcastle United 2
Wimbledon 0
Premier League, St. James' Park, August 21st, 1996

"My home debut, my first goal for Newca – it was all there, wasn't it. I was so keer mark my home debut for the club with a goal and with four minutes to go and us ahead we got a free-kick outside the box the Leazes End. I curled it over the wall into the far corner. Given the occasion, a the goal, that put the Wimbledon game up there for me."

wcastle United 2
ttenham Hotspur 0
Cup Semi-Final, Old Trafford,
ril 11th, 1999

'd beaten Sheffield United the previous year
e same stage and at the same venue, but
respect to Sheffield United Tottenham were
er and stronger opponents. It was a
endous battle in a great atmosphere which
into extra time and then I got a penalty
wed by a shot from the edge of the box
h is one of my own favourite goals."

er-Milan 2
wcastle United 2
mpions League, San Siro Stadium
rch 12th, 2003

picked this one as one of the best because
many things – the occasion, the superb
nd, and best of all those 15,000 Newcastle
orters behind the goal. It really was a
omenal sight. And the fact that I got a
e of good goals in a good result – a 2-2
– all added to it. It was so special, and a
when Newcastle United matched one of
nest teams in Europe.

wcastle United 5
nchester United 0
mier League, St. James' Park,
ber 20th, 1996

is many fans' favourite, and it's one of
, too, though not the tops. We'd been beaten
title by Manchester United the season
e, we'd been beaten 4-0 by them at
bley in the Charity Shield, but on the day at
mes' we destroyed them and gave our fans
thing special to remember. I scored one,
n Peacock, Les Ferdinand, David Ginola
f course Philippe Albert with that brilliant
t the end got the goals and people still talk
it now."

Newcastle United 1
Sheffield United 0
FA Cup Semi-Final,
Old Trafford,
April 5th, 1998

"The atmosphere was
fantastic and Sheffield United
gave us a really hard fight but
I scored the only goal with a
follow-up after the keeper
saved my header. I had family
in the big stand where there
were 20,000 Geordies on the
far side and they and others
told me that the stand was
literally shaking!"

Newcastle United 4
Leicester City 3
Premier League,
St. James' Park,
February 2nd, 1997

"We were 3-1 down with not
long left and then I got the
quickest hat-trick of my career – one, two,
three in the space of 13 minutes to turn it
round and win 4-3. The excitement at the end
was something else. It started with a free-kick
and ended with a tap-in in the 90th minute,
and what a memorable finish that was."

Newcastle United 8
Sheffield Wednesday 0
Premier League, St. James' Park,
September 19th, 1999

Because of the circumstances leading up to
that game, with the Ruud Gullit thing and me
being left out against Sunderland, scoring five
goals was a statement from me. It was also
Bobby Robson's first home game in charge of
Newcastle after coming in as manager, and
re-launched our season." Five goals was great
for me, and 8-0 was great for everybody."

Newcastle United 3
Bayer Leverkusen 1
Champions League, St. James' Park,
February 26th, 2003

"It might not have been the greatest of games, but
because it was the Champions League my hat-trick was
something of an achievement, as not everyone gets a
hat-trick in Europe's biggest competition. It's the best
there is – so to get three goals made it extra-special."

"And there were others that were special for me,
too. I'm thinking in particular of the Champions
League win away to Feyenoord in 2002-03, when
we won 3-2 with a last-minute goal to go
through to the second stage.

"And there was the Stevenage FA Cup-tie in
'98, when I scored one down there and two in the
replay at St. James' after being out for six
months with that serious ankle injury.

"The Charlton home game in April 2002, when
I got my 200th Premier League goal, also stands
out in my mind.

"And of course there was the Sunderland
game which turned out to be my last one, and
for which the goal was one of my top ones.

"But these nine games are my favourite ones
for Newcastle United."

15

...and my top nine Newcastle goals

Alan Shearer ended his Newcastle United career with 206 goals in 404 appearances – a tremendous record and one which brought him the honour of becoming the club's all-time top scorer.

But which are Alan's favourite black-and-white goals?

Here, he picks out his own top nine ... and reserves a special mention for the 206th and last.

GOAL! 1

GOAL! 173

EVERTON
Premier League, St. James' Park,
December 1st 2002. 2-1

"Technically, this one has to be at the top of the list ever_ time. It was the volley from a knock-on by Shola and wh_ was just pot luck whether it went in, I have to say I did c_ as sweet as a nut and it flew in perfectly, giving the goalkeeper no chance from way outside the box. We ha_ behind in the game a long time, and it was late in the g_ when I equalised, but after I scored we got another and 2-1."

CHELSEA
Premier League, St. James' Park,
April 25th, 2004. 2-1

"This was another long-range one, and not too far behi_ Everton goal. I turned Marcel Desailly 25 yards out and soon as the shot left my boot it was heading for the stanchion. The keeper knew he was beaten, too – it's a feeling when you hit one and know straight away that it going in. And I knew that one was going in."

ASTON VILLA
Premier League, St. James' Park,
November 3rd, 2001. 3-0

"Rob Lee's always said he made this goal with a great for it was his diagonal ball that reached me at the back penalty area. But it was a good pass, not a great pass! was no-one in the box so I reckoned it was worth just a go, and my volley flew straight across Peter Schmeic_ the far corner. It was the look on Schmeichel's face tha_ helped make it even more memorable!"

TOTTENHAM HOTSPUR

**Premier League, St. James' Park,
December 28th, 1996. 7-1.**

"This was a different sort of goal, as I had to go past a number of defenders before shooting. The ball was played long and headed on, and I was pushing past defenders and finally was left with the keeper ahead of me. Rather than blast it, I placed it into the top corner – with power!"

TOTTENHAM HOTSPUR

**FA Cup Semi-Final, Old Trafford,
April 11th, 1999. 2-0.**

"We had gone into extra time at Old Trafford and I'd already scored a penalty from handball against Sol Campbell when we got another build-up on the left. I fed Silvio Maric and he squared it back to me. From just outside the box I shot first-time, cutting across the ball. As soon as it left my right foot I knew it was going in. Ian Walker, the Spurs goalkeeper, made an effort but had no chance. And what made it all the better was the knowledge that we were heading for Wembley again."

ARSENAL

**Premier League, St. James' Park,
May 14th, 2000**

"This one was a free-kick at the Leazes End in the final game of the season. Arsenal had just equalised to make it 1-1 when we got the free-kick, Arsenal lined up the wall, and I went for it – the shot passed through the wall and was still rising when it hit the top corner, beating Alex Manninger all ends up. It was also my 300th career goal."

GOAL! 130

15

MBLEDON

**mier League, St. James' Park,
ust 21st, 1996**

as my Newcastle home debut, which added e occasion, but technically this was also a good goal. We got a free-kick well to the left al outside the area, and I had to bend it up ver the wall and into the far corner. Which I wanted a goal to mark my home debut, this t, and I was chuffed with it both for what it and what it meant on such an occasion."

NCHESTER UNITED

**mier League, Old Trafford,
ember 23rd, 2002**

her free-kick, and another special one. It strange game, with some strange goals, lon't think there was anything too strange this one. It was 25 yards out, the ball got ed to me, and I caught it perfectly. The ball nto the top right corner past Fabien Barthez 100th Premier League goal for Newcastle."

SHEFFIELD UNITED

**FA Cup Semi-Final, Old Trafford,
April 5th, 1998**

"This may not have looked like a great goal to everybody, but in my view it was a real poacher's goal. It was a good cross from 'Digger' Barnes and I got the header in which 'Paddy' Kelly, the Sheffield United keeper, half-saved. The defender had gone to ground but I'd kept my feet and was able to get in ahead of another defender to get to the ball. It was about an inch off the line when I stuck it in – and I'm lethal from that distance!"

"And others?
"Well, I have to say that that penalty at Sunderland, my very last goal in my final game, is a special one for me, even if it was just a penalty. Having missed one six years earlier against Sunderland at St. James', I really wanted to score this one. And I didn't even think of missing it. I knew where I was putting it and in it went. The keeper was never going to save it ..."

Same old Shearer

Always pouring...

ALAN SHEARER
the ultimate ambassador

BARRY MOAT, CHAIRMAN, ALAN SHEARER TESTIMONIAL COMMITTEE

PAUL MORAN · ANDY NAYLOR · BARRY MOAT · KENNETH SHEPHERD · HELENE HOLLIER · ROBIN WINSKELL · CHARLOTTE SWANN

ALAN SHEARER TESTIMONIAL COMMITTEE

(COMMITTEE MEMBER SIMON BAYLIFF ABSENT FROM PICTURE)

BEHALF OF THE ALAN SHEARER TIMONIAL COMMITTEE I would like elcome you all to what is bound to one of the most emotionally-rged nights ever witnessed here at James' Park ... the night when for very last time we will have the ilege of paying tribute to Alan packed stadium.

ey say that you always remember historical s and they do not come any more special to a castle United fan than 29th July 1996: the hat "Shearer came home" for a then world rd transfer fee of £15m ... undoubtedly the pound for pound signing the club has ever e.

an would not swap any amount of medals for t he believes he has benefited from by being for the last 10 years of his career.

e chance to bring "home" his lovely wife ya and children and allow them to grow up ngst his own close family and friends in rcastle, the place closest to his heart, and to in front of "his" people week in week out ... is what is important to Alan Shearer, that is rue mark of his character.

an has been the ultimate ambassador, not for the football club but also for the City and eople of Newcastle throughout his rious career, and he is joined here tonight by e other great servants to the club to play for one very last time. His close friends Rob, , Les and Steve will join Alan in his nsong here tonight at St. James' and I am you will give them all a very special Geordie ome home.

has been my huge honour and privilege to be monial Committee Chairman, not only

because of my respect for and friendship with the man but also to operate alongside my colleagues on his committee who have worked so incredibly hard along with club staff to pull these events together; and to whom Alan offers his heartfelt thanks.

As many of you will already be aware, Alan has made the decision to - in his words - "give something back" to the people of the North-East by donating the entire proceeds of his testimonial to charitable causes within the area: yet another shining example of the man and the legend.

Once again, we offer you sincere thanks for coming along to this very special evening, and hope you enjoy every moment of the occasion.

Even though Alan, sadly, will be unable to play this evening due to a knee injury, everyone here will be able to pay their final tributes to our greatest-ever goalscorer, and arguably our greatest-ever player.

How fitting it was that Alan's final deed was to score for United in a derby victory against local rivals Sunderland.

Tonight, the stage belongs to Alan Shearer and I'm sure that every one of the Toon Army will remind him that in our hearts he is and always will be "England's Number One".

Let's give Alan a night to remember.

**BARRY MOAT, Chairman,
Alan Shearer Testimonial Committee**

HE LORD MAYOR OF NEWCASTLE

On behalf of the City I am delighted to congratulate Alan Shearer on an outstanding career both on and off the pitch.

When Alan signed for Newcastle in 1996 he could have gone anywhere in the world to play football, but he chose to come home and dedicate the rest of his playing career to Newcastle United.

His commitment and dedication to football and Newcastle United has made him a hero not only in his home city, but also around the world.

During his time as captain of England, Alan was an excellent ambassador for the country and has represented Newcastle on an international stage.

It was this commitment to football which earned him the OBE in the Queen's Birthday Honours in 2001.

Alan has always been keen to support many worthy causes, both locally and nationally, and I would like to thank him for his generosity by continuing to support the Lord Mayor's official charity.

In 2000 Alan was awarded the City's highest honour, the Honorary Freedom of Newcastle upon Tyne.

He shares this honour with another Newcastle United legend, Jackie Millburn, whose goalscoring record he broke earlier this year, an achievement I along with my colleagues on Newcastle City Council and the people of Newcastle would like to congratulate him on.

This record, I am sure, will remain on Newcastle United's record books for a very long time.

As he heads toward his retirement from football Alan's legacy will go on to inspire the footballing stars of the future and hopefully this will produce another record scoring hero.

It just remains for me to say that I wish Alan and his family well for the future and I hope he continues to play a role in the life of Newcastle.

Councillor David Slesenger
The Lord Mayor of Newcastle

19

Home is where the heart lies

Many people have played a part in the football life of Alan Shearer, but no-one has played a greater part than **Jack Hixon**.

Jack is the scout who discovered Shearer, the mentor who launched him on his career at Southampton, the advisor who guided him through, and today, at 85, the friend who still talks to his one-time protégé almost daily.

Few, other than Alan's own family, are closer to the legend. But, there again, Jack is as family to Shearer.

He knows the Geordie passion that courses through Alan's veins and says that even when he was putting the 14-year-old on the bus to the south coast outside the Pilgrim Street Odeon in Newcastle in 1984, he knew deep down that one day he would come back to Tyneside.

"It's where the heart lies," Jack says. "People go on glibly about the silverware Alan didn't get at Newcastle United, but it's a case of home being where the heart lies.

"It was destiny that he would come back here eventually. He's a Gallowgate Ender who identifies with the fans here, and the fans identify with him. Alan Shearer is part and parcel of Newcastle United.

"I always felt that he would come back to Newcastle one day, although that was something I had no influence over. But I knew that if the opportunity arose, and if there were options, this would be the track he would take.

"He could never have had at any other club what he has had here at Newcastle United. It's a personal relationship with the Geordies, a personal relationship with the 52,000 who come to St. James' Park every other week. He's Wor Al, he's Big Al – and he couldn't get that anywhere else.

" 'Wor' says he belongs up here. It's like heritage. He's a man of the people – a part of us.

"Ruud van Nistelrooy cannot get this at Manchester United, for example, as he's not a local hero. Wayne Rooney doesn't get it at Manchester United, because he's from Liverpool. But Alan is a Geordie among Geordies."

OFF TO THE DEEP SOUTH

It is almost 22 years since Jack joined Alan's parents Alan and Anne at the bus stop outside the Odeon in the centre of Newcastle to set the young Shearer off on his football career.

The young hopeful had to change at Victoria in London to carry on to Southampton where a Geordie whom Saints scout Jack had taken to Burnley in 1960 was waiting to welcome the new intake of youngsters.

Dave Merrington took Shearer and others under his wing and quickly saw and developed the raw talent into something even more potent.

By 1988 Merrington was urging the then-Saints manager, Chris Nicholl, to put the 17-year-old Shearer in the side; Nicholl, to his credit, did exactly that.

Jack, having watched Berwick Rangers lose 2-0 at home to St. Johnstone on a

scouting mission, was driving out of the border town at five o'clock on the Saturday evening of April 9th 1988 when he reached for the car radio controls to switch on Radio Five.

The familiar strains of Sports Report faded to the presenter reading the football headlines ... and the big news of the day. A Kid Called Shearer Had Scored A Hat-Trick Against Arsenal At the Dell.

"And I nearly swerved into a ditch," smiles Jack. "You couldn't have expected that on Alan's first full start. But that was some start, wasn't it.

"It was fantastic – but the problem Southampton then had was that Alan hadn't actually signed a contract at that stage and the hat-trick alerted all the clubs.

"Chris Nicholl had to make Alan an offer and get him signed up in a hurry as Newcastle were one of the clubs interested.

"Alan phoned me and I wrote down what I thought he should ask for and posted it down to him. When he sat down with Chris Nicholl three days after the Arsenal game, Chris was surprised that a young lad had everything written down in front of him that he wanted to ask for.

"So Chris asked to see the piece of paper, and he would have recognised my handwriting had Alan taken in my notes with him. But he'd been wise enough to write it all out himself in his own handwriting ... and he got the deal!"

LOYALTY AND RESPECT

Alan went on to build a major reputation at Southampton and in 1992 commanded a British record £3.6m fee when he moved to Blackburn Rovers.

Three years later he played a more-than-significant role in helping Kenny Dalglish's Blackburn side to the Premier League title, and Alan, by now a regular England international, was the star Jack Hixon had seen in embryo a decade earlier.

The respect Shearer held for Dalglish and many others, says Jack, was typical of the man. For respect and loyalty have always figured large in his character.

"Alan is very loyal and very faithful," he says. "He's been loyal to people who have taken care of him, he's been loyal to his clubs, and he's been very loyal to Jack Hixon. We've never lost touch, and he once said of me: 'He's family'. What greater accolade can anyone give?

"Alan has given me his England shirt from his last Wembley appearance. I've got his Newcastle shirt from when they played Tottenham in the Cup. I've got his Youth shirt. The memorabilia he's given me shows a real affinity.

"He gave me that Wembley shirt when I was in hospital. Kevin Keegan was the England manager and they were due to go to Malta but Kevin allowed Alan to fly back to Newcastle to visit me before they travelled.

"Alan came in to Rake Lane Hospital and they brought him in via the fire escape. And he brought that shirt – which, he warned me, was stinking! The actual word he used was 'humming'. But I treasured it and kept it – sweat and everything!"

Adds Jack: "That spoke volumes for the man. Ability can take you to the top but it's character that keeps you there. And Shearer has character.

"We differ in our opinions sometimes, and rightly so. But we respect each other's opinions. And Alan has respect for people – respect for the person and the position that person holds.

"He's articulate, but never talks down to people, which is an art in itself; and not a developed art. I think it's inherent in the man. And it goes back to respect.

Jack watched Shearer develop from an early age and made contact with his parents – a contact that became lifelong friendship. Scout and father drink together as pals each and every week.

Jack says: "Even when Alan was playing for Newcastle Under-13s and I approached his father, he said 'you had better speak to him'. That was the measure of the young Alan Shearer – everything about the fella exuded confidence in his own ability.

"The family was always totally supportive, but advisory. And there was never anything precocious about Alan. He was just sound, and always got on with it and did his best.

"His parents were always there to offer advice but his father never intruded. He's a very shy and circumspect fella, but with immense pride in what his son has done – as has his mother."

THE GREATEST OF THEM ALL

It is on the field, of course, that Alan Shearer has written the story of his glorious career.

And ever since Jack almost ended up in a ditch at the side of the A1 18 years ago, he has watched his protégé develop into an international superstar.

As one of the few who saw Hughie Gallacher play still around to tell the tale, and as one who has admired the power and glory of Jackie Milburn, Malcolm Macdonald, Wyn Davies et al since, Jack Hixon is well-qualified to judge the merits of the various Newcastle United No. 9 heroes.

And he says: "I loved Jackie and all he did, both as a player and a person. But to me Alan is top man.

"I saw Gallacher when I was a youngster, and I saw Milburn and all the rest at Newcastle. I saw the Lawtons and the Lofthouses and the Linekers playing for other clubs.

"And I can confidently say Shearer is the best in my time – the best at the job he does.

"When he was brought to Newcastle by Kevin Keegan in 1996, Newcastle had just missed out on the Championship and I, like many others, believed Shearer would be the final piece in the jigsaw and that Newcastle would win the title the next year, 1996-97.

"When they paired Shearer up with players like Ferdinand, and Beardsley, and Lee, and all those other quality players in the Newcastle team of '96, you had the belief that Alan would make the difference in winning the title.

"Alan wasn't a gamble. Even at a world record £15m Alan was no gamble. How many records has he destroyed? How many goals has he scored? How many more goals has he created?

"The Championship didn't happen, of course, for whatever reasons – but I still come back to my point that despite that, Alan has had something at Newcastle United that he couldn't have had anywhere else.

"He is a born leader – he has captained every side he has played in. And whatever you might say about his technical qualities - you may say he's a little bit short on his left foot, for example – the great thing about him is his sheer presence.

"When he walks out of the tunnel he exudes presence. People use the phrase 'born leader' glibly, but if I was in trouble I would want Shearer at my side ... and I know I would get total honesty and total loyalty."

AND FINALLY ...

So, as Jack Hixon sits in the Milburn Stand at St. James' Park tonight watching Alan Shearer bid farewell to his playing days, what emotions will he feel?

"I think I will feel a sense of deprivation," Jack says with honesty. "We will be losing his presence on the field.

"Alan has run the course and you cannot take that away from him. But I will feel that we have got a void I cannot see ever being filled.

"I would hope Michael Owen would go a long way towards compensating for the loss of Alan Shearer.

"There may be others who come in. Who knows? But we will miss Shearer, without a doubt.

"He is unique, and irreplaceable."

"Every time we got the ball, we just gave it to Alan because we knew he would score."

MIKE NEWELL pays tribute to his former strike partner from the Ewood Park days – though, tongue-in-cheek, he says Alan Shearer was hard work as a room-mate...

"Four of the hardest years of my life were spent at Blackburn when I roomed with Alan Shearer.

"He is the most boring man in the world.

"People have this picture of Alan when they see him in interviews, when he comes across all sensible and straight-laced and never smiles.

"Well, that's what he's like away from the cameras as well.

"I'm only joking, of course. Away from the cameras and the spotlight, Alan really is one of the lads and he has a great sense of humour.

"He hadn't really made his name when he joined us at Blackburn, and to be honest he didn't have a very good pre-season. A few of the lads were saying 'oh aye, three million for this fella?'

"But in the first game away at Crystal Palace, he scored two belters and they will stay with me for a long time. I can still picture them now, and that was the moment he arrived as far as I'm concerned.

"He basically made an immediate impact that day, not just for Blackburn Rovers but for the Premier League as well.

"In those first six months, before he did his knee in on Boxing Day, he was as strong as anyone I've ever seen.

"He was absolutely uncontainable. He wasn't the quickest, but once he got into his stride there was no stopping him. He would just shrug defenders off.

"Every time we got the ball, we just gave it to Alan because we knew he would score. Most of the time he did, and the people that used to back him to score the first goal every week must have made a fortune.

"He was a great player to play alongside. I considered myself to be an average player, but playing alongside him made you look better. Not just me, but whoever partnered him up front.

"I could talk all day about some of the goals he has scored. One away to QPR stands out, he just smashed this ball from about 25 or 30 yards and it flew in. No goalkeeper in the world would have stopped it.

"I remember his goal against Everton for Newcastle as well. I was manager of Hartlepool at the time, and I was on my way to the North East Football Writers' Dinner when my dad rang me and told me I just had to see this goal that Shearer had scored.

"I couldn't wait to get to the hotel to see it on the telly – and I wasn't disappointed.

"I don't think I have ever seen anyone hit a ball as hard as he did. We used to call him club foot, because of his left foot.

"It wasn't bad, but he just used to swing it in the box and see what happened. He has the heaviest legs and feet in the world, they are like lead weights.

"I wish Alan all the very best on his big night, and it didn't really surprise me that the game sold out weeks ago.

"I don't think he'll be out of the game for too long, and I'm sure he will want to put something back in.

"It wouldn't surprise me if he ends up managing Newcastle United one day, I don't think he is the sort of character who would need to learn his trade in the lower leagues.

"He didn't win anything as a player with Newcastle – but I'd love to see him do it as their manager.

"All the best Al."

"HE HAS THIS HUGE MENTAL STRENGTH, THIS INNER BELIEF IN HIMSELF"

TIM FLOWERS has spent many a training session picking the ball out of the back of his net during the time he spent with Alan at Southampton and Blackburn. But one training session in particular stands out for the former England international...

"Alan is a bit younger than me, and I recall a session at Southampton where the first team were playing the kids.

"I was in the Reserves at the time, but Peter Shilton wasn't training for some reason so I was in goal for the first team that day.

"This ball has been knocked through, and this kid with big hairy legs stuck on a boy's body came running in to get on the end of it.

"I bent down to scoop it up, and bang, this kid came right through me and completely cleaned me out. We ended up rolling around brawling after that one.

"That was Alan Shearer. The legs haven't changed, but his body has got bigger,

"It was obvious he had a special talent when he was at Southampton, he was basically fast-tracked through the Reserves and into the first team. As everyone knows, he scored a hat-trick on his debut against Arsenal – what a debut that was!

"He moved up to Blackburn before me, and when I signed for them he helped me find a house and settle in and all that sort of stuff.

"We used to share lifts to training, me, him and Mike Newell. I'm sure he used to charge us when it was his turn to drive, but he always has been as tight as a camel's backside in a sandstorm.

"One day they both brought their cars to my house, and jumped in mine to go to training.

"I had just bought this big Land Rover Discovery, and I came out from training and the car was gone.I was fuming, I honestly thought it had been nicked. I had a major panic on.

"It eventually turned out that those two had moved it, and parked it up by this old folks' home near where we used to train.

"I didn't see the funny side to be honest, and I remember driving back just blanking them, with Shearer and Newell just tittering away in the back seat. I had the real hump with them.

"That was typical of them, though - particularly Alan. You'd come in and find your suit with half an arm on and all that sort of stuff.

"The night we won the title at Anfield, we went back to this bistro in Preston. It was one of those gaffes where you have the meal and a few drinks, listen to the live band, then get up and dance on the tables.

"I'm sure Alan was there that night – and round at my house the next day when we had a few drinks prior to taking the trophy to Ewood - so I don't know where that tale in his book about him creosoting his garden fence instead of partying came from.

"But I tell you what, he knew when to cut out the daft stuff and focus on the game.

"He has this huge mental strength, this inner belief in himself. He's not arrogant, it is just an unbelievable strength of his. You can't captain your country without that, can you?

"He has had it right through his career, right back to those training sessions in the early days at Southampton.

"He's had a great career, with goals all the way through, though if I remember rightly he's only put a couple past me down the years.

"Even though he can't play, I hope he has a great night to cap off a great career this evening."

23

POLAR®

LISTEN TO YOUR BODY

SHEARER ... the ultimate professional on and off the field

Sir John Hall was Chairman of Newcastle United when Alan Shearer signed for a then world record fee of £15m from Blackburn Rovers.

It was July 1996, and the move heralded a new era in United's history even as they developed into a major football force.

Assessing the impact Shearer has had on the club and the region, Sir John says: "Alan Shearer is the ultimate professional on and off the pitch, he has played for England, and everything he has done for Newcastle United and England has brought credit on this club.

"He has been a great ambassador for the club. He is probably at this moment the player that all fans recognise throughout the world.

"We have all the wonderful treasure-chest of memories of the Shearer years, just as in the past we had wonderful memories of the Milburn years, and the Macdonald years; even the Keegan years.

"Number Nines at Newcastle United are always special, but in his own era, Alan Shearer has become a major part of the history of Newcastle United Football Club – and he is a legend.

"The stories will continue to be written about him and in the future people of my generation will tell their grandchildren: 'Oh, you should have seen Shearer'.

"Off the pitch, Alan Shearer has also done many things for the club. He has consolidated season-ticket sales, he has attracted sponsors, he has become a symbol of Newcastle. He has been an entire package.

"Back in 1996, the club had no misgivings at all about paying such a lot of money to bring him here from Blackburn Rovers. The Board has supported every manager with money for players, and we supported Kevin Keegan then with the money to buy Shearer.

"Undoubtedly, Alan has been value for money – in fact, I wish we could have had a lot more Alan Shearers.

"We all come to the end of our time at some stage – all of us. But life will go on after Alan has gone, and there will be other players who come along to fill Alan's place.

"That is both a curse and a blessing. Anyone who tries to be Alan Shearer Mark II would be daft. For there can be no Alan Shearer Mark II. Anyone who follows Shearer will have to be their own man. But anyone who follows him and achieves anything like his success will be a new hero.

"To Alan himself, on behalf of Lady Hall and myself, I say: 'Thanks, young man'. For Alan is still a young man with most of his life before him.

"He now has to assess and decide what he is going to do in the future, but I am sure he will be a success whatever he does.

"And if he decides to go into management, I have no doubt that with his temperament and knowledge of the game, he will prove to be a first-class manager."

Made in Heaven

The magnificent partnership of Alan Shearer and Les Ferdinand at Newcastle United in 1996-97 was, in the view of many good experts, the greatest twin spearhead of them all.

It yielded 49 goals between them in a campaign that ended in Champions League qualification from second place, and is remembered more than fondly by all Newcastle fans.

For Les, who was at United a year before Alan arrived, it was the final piece in the jigsaw – and although the title remained just out of reach for the second year in succession, there wasn't a team in the country that could match the Shearer-Ferdinand goals combo.

Les will play this evening when he lines up in the United team to take on Celtic – one of Alan's special guests in his testimonial line-up.

And the years will roll back ... even to that famous day in July 1996 when the United squad was boarding the plane to the Far East, and manager Kevin Keegan was getting off.

Says Les: "I always remember Kevin getting off that plane, and we knew something big was going on.

"We didn't know it was Alan at that time, but later Kevin told first Peter Beardsley, as captain, and then myself, as the guy who was going to play alongside Alan.

"Kevin told me: 'We are signing Alan Shearer tomorrow', and I said just one word: 'Brilliant.'

"During the previous season Kevin had said to me that he thought we needed another top forward alongside me and when he said it was going to be Alan Shearer I thought: 'That's exactly what we need – they don't come any better than that!'

"Mind you, some people reckoned me and Alan wouldn't be able to play together. They said we were too similar – both target men. But the fact is that Alan was great at moving around into different positions and together we proved the doubters wrong.

"When I was at Queen's Park Rangers I also used to roam round different parts of the pitch, so we both knew about going into different areas rather than just being target men around the opposition box.

"We had to work at it a little bit at first, but then it just clicked. And it wasn't about how many goals we were each going to score – whether Alan was going to get more than Les, or whether Les was going to get more than Alan. It was just playing as a partnership for Newcastle United, and when we counted the goals up there were 49 of them between us.

"And it was an absolute pleasure. The way it worked out, I became more of a target man, and Alan moved around more, but it still enabled me to do what I did at QPR and go into different areas of the pitch.

"We mustn't forget the great players like Rob Lee and Peter Beardsley that we had behind us supplying the ball – they were marvellous, and the goals were just flying in. When you look back at the videos of that season, it's fantastic to see. It's only a pity it didn't last longer.

"I say without hesitation that Alan Shearer was the best striker I ever played with. His single-mindedness was phenomenal, and his record proves his quality. We had a brilliant understanding – I knew where to go when he went up to flick a ball on, and he knew where to go when I went for the ball.

"It all came to a peak in that Manchester United game, when we won 5-0 at St. James' in October '96 – by then it was total football, and what we produced on that day was marvellous to

Les, to the disappointment of many, was sold to Tottenham Hotspur on the eve of the 1997-98 season – barely a day before Alan shattered his ankle in a pre-season tournament at Everton. Suddenly, the partnership was gone, and United were never quite the same again.

Les believes, though, that had he and Shearer continued to play together for that second season and more, the partnership would have stepped up to yet another level – if that were possible.

"I think without a shadow of doubt that we would have been able to repeat it – at least," Les says. "Alan and I had learned a lot about each other in that first season together and I believe we could have been even better in 1997-98.

"I was really looking forward to the start of that season and getting going, but then I was sold and Alan got injured, and that was it. One very, very good year together – one never to be forgotten."

Off the field, Les knew Alan as a different man to that projected by his TV image.

"He comes across as very dour on television," says Les, "but he's not like that when you get to know him.

"Alan and David Batty used to get up to all sorts of mischief, and he was a great character that I got on really well with.

"Playing alongside Alan again tonight would have been a privilege and an honour. I was only at Newcastle for two years, and only one of those was with Alan – but those years were fabulous, really fabulous."

Alan Shearer

Testimonial 2006

BACK DETAIL

TESTIMONIAL T-SHIRT
Sizes: SB, MB, LB, XLB
Price: £7.00
Sizes: S, M, L, XL, XXL
Price: £10.00

SHEARER LIMITED EDITION

SHEARER LIMITED EDITION MP3 PLAYER
128MB Memory
holds up to 60 songs.
Also includes a recorded
message from Alan Shearer
Price: £21.00

TESTIMONIAL MUG
Price: £5.00

TESTIMONIAL FLAG
Price: £8.00

TESTIMONIAL SCARF
Price: £6.00

TESTIMONIAL T-SHIRT
Sizes: S, M, L, XL, XXL, XX
Price: £45.00

OPTIONAL TESTIMONIAL NAME & NUMBER £10

Available Exclusively from Official Club Stores at
St. James' Park, Monument Mall, Eldon Square & Metro Centre
NUFC Direct 0870 442 1892   Shop On-line www.nufc.co.uk

NEWCASTLE UNITED

Thanks for 10 great years

chael Owen looked to Alan Shearer for
spiration when he burst onto the
gland scene, and eight years later he
kindled that partnership in the black and
ite stripes of Newcastle United. United's
cord signing is full of praise for a man
o also held that honour when he moved
Gallowgate a decade ago.

'Alan was a big help to me when I came
ough into the England team, and we have
t on well ever since then," Michael says.
"Obviously he is a lot older than me, but we
ve struck up a friendship and we share a lot
common interests.

"Alan was very persuasive in getting me to
n for Newcastle, he painted a great picture
the club and the city and as everyone
ows, he was a big factor in me moving to
e club.

"In the games we played together, it didn't
ke long to rekindle that partnership, and it's
great shame that my injury in December and

his injury last month meant we couldn't
have got a few more games together.

"But from Alan's point of view, if you're
going to go out with two goals in your last
home game, then an important goal in the
derby away to your arch-rivals, then he
probably couldn't have asked for a better
way to finish."

Adds Michael: "We have had some great
games together, and a lot of happy memories.

"I knew he was a popular figure up here, but
you don't realise just how much he means to
the people until you actually get involved with
the club.

"And I have also witnessed what it means
for Alan to play for his own public. The
celebrations after he scored the goal that
broke the record will live long in the memory.

"It doesn't surprise me that his testimonial
game sold out as quickly as it did. It's a
measure of the man that people queued up
overnight just to get their hands on a seat for
tonight's match.

"The tribute banner on the back of the stand
is a tremendous honour for him as well.

"I drove up to St. James' the other week
when it had just been unfurled, and it was
actually quite an emotional moment to see it,
thanking him for his 10 years at the club.

"That just shows what people think of him,
and it wouldn't have happened to any other
player.

"I have no doubts that his testimonial game
will be a fitting tribute to Alan, and I'm sure it
will prove to be an unforgettable night that is
fully deserved."

LAINYA SHEARER

LIFE AS THE WIFE OF A SOCCER SUPERSTAR

The first time Alan Shearer met his wife-to-be Lainya, they were both teenagers in a Southampton bar. And she bought the drinks. **"Well, he was a £40-a-week trainee and I had a full-time job,"** Lainya says. **"So I bought him his drink!"**

These days, Alan can better afford to buy the drinks, but fame and fortune has not changed the nature either of him or Lainya in the near-two decades since.

They are still the down-to-earth couple who enjoy the benefits of wealth without being altered by it. "Alan hasn't changed at all since those days," Lainya says, "and nor have I. We are still the same as we were then.

"The way people treat Alan now is different – to them, he's a great footballer, he's famous, he's a hero. And yes, he is all of those things.

"But as a person he is no different, and neither am I. He has become older, he has achieved his ambitions, we live in a lovely house ... but because Alan is the way he is, we have stayed just the way we always were.

"Some people have a need to be famous, and fame can make you a different person. But that has never happened to us. We have always been very similar in the way we look at life and in the way we want to bring up the children

"I'm a very laid-back person – calm and laid-back. I just like to be me, and I don't want to change."

At a time when the public perception of footballers' wives has been shaped by an extravagant TV series of the same name, Lainya Shearer is the opposite – loyal, quiet and determinedly anonymous.

Alan has protected his family from the glare of publicity over the years, not least Lainya and their children Chloe, 13, Hollie, 11, and Will, five.

As a result, if Lainya walks down the street by herself she goes unnoticed by the public. If she and Alan walk down the same street together, they are repeatedly stopped by United supporters anxious to talk football with the man who has become a Tyneside icon.

Lainya accepts the situation and says: "People don't know me. I think if you are not in the paper, people are not looking for you, and I am not in the paper.

"If we walk down the street together, we get stopped. If I walk down the street by myself, no-one knows me. And we are happy to have it that way.

"I'm still the same as I was when I first met Alan. I know that's probably hard to believe, but it's true. And Alan hasn't changed either."

Lainya was never a football fan before meeting and marrying Alan, and even now she admits she is far from a fanatic – although she does enjoy watching games.

She admits: "I was never a football fan before I met and married Alan, and even now I wouldn't put the TV on to watch, say, Chelsea v Liverpool, although Alan would.

"I love going to games and watching Alan play, and so do the children. And if he's not playing, we still go and want the team to win.

"But I don't think I've ever become a real football fan – although the kids certainly have!"

FOLLOWING THE STAR

When Lainya married Alan at St. James' Church in Southampton on June 8th, 1991, she knew she could in all probability be committing herself to a life away from her family in Southampton.

Sure enough, as Alan's fame grew, a move away from the south coast became increasingly inevitable, and when he moved to Blackburn Rovers in the summer of 1992, Lainya knew she was leaving her Hampshire home never to return.

Southampton-born and bred, and lovingly close to her family, she says now: "We knew the day that I left Southampton that I would never go home.

"Alan and I come from two different ends of the country and we always knew I would end up where he played last, which now is Newcastle.

"I have supported him wherever he went, wherever he chose to play his football, and, being honest, it hasn't always been easy. When we moved to Blackburn I found it different and hard to settle, and when we came to Newcastle I found it even more different – and, at first, very hard to adjust.

"When we went to Blackburn I had just had a baby – Chloe, our eldest – and it was a case of a baby and a suitcase. My mam and dad, Gen and Steve, were fantastic – they used to come up all the time to help.

"But I said to Alan: 'You have to play your football, so I will go wherever you go'.

"When you have to decide which way to go, what decision to make, something guides you. It's a gut feeling – and Alan's gut feeling hasn't let him down so far."

Adds Lainya: "Now I can honestly say we are very, very, very happy here. Newcastle is a great city, and I think the people are great. Southampton as a city has pretty well everything, but it doesn't have the buzz that Newcastle has.

"We have our favourite restaurants where we eat out, we have good friends, but if we go, say, to the theatre, we tend to go to London because you can be more anonymous there."

Fame came gradually upon Alan. After bursting onto the scene with a debut hat-trick for Southampton against Arsenal at The Dell in April 1988, his subsequent progress was steady rather than spectacular for a year or two. But by the time he joined Blackburn for a British record fee in the summer of '92, he was a big name with a big reputation for scoring goals.

Three years later, Blackburn won the Premier League title, and Alan hit over 30 goals in three successive campaigns – the only Premier League player ever to do so.

Then, in 1996, he commanded a world record fee of £15m when he joined his home-town club Newcastle United – and the rest is history.

Lainya looks back over the past two decades and says: "Alan became famous gradually. Today he's very

"LIKE MOST FOOTBALLERS, HE JUST LIVED TO PLAY. SO WHEN THEY CAN'T PLAY, THEY GET FRUSTRATED. AND ALAN GOT VERY FRUSTRATED."

famous, but it has happened very gradually to us, so we've had a lot of time to grow with it and get used to it.

"It hasn't been an overnight thing. We didn't wake up one morning and find that Alan was suddenly famous.

"It's probably right to say that the children have never known anything different to their father being very famous, but Alan's relationship to them, and to me, is very close and loving – like any good father and husband.

"He takes the children to school, he is a very good father in every way, and they all love him dearly. The girls used to kick a ball around with him, and Will, who is five now, loves to play with him. When Alan goes out to training in the morning, Will will say to him: `Are we playing golf or football tonight, daddy?'"

After Chloe and Holly, Lainya and Alan always planned a third child, although whether boy or girl was not a major consideration.

Lainya adds: "It wasn't something that we talked about, really. We had the two girls and we wanted another child. It was always going to be three children for us.

"If it was a boy, then great, but we were definitely not particularly going for a boy. However, Alan and his dad were pleased when it was a boy – and Alan's dad is certainly now a very proud grandad!"

THOSE INJURY NIGHTMARES

It's one thing having a happy and successful footballer husband doing his stuff out on the playing field week after week. But it's altogether another having a husband laid up with serious injury and kicking the metaphorical cat in his frustration at not being able to get out there and play.

Lainya Shearer has experienced that three times for long periods – once at Blackburn, and twice at Newcastle, and it was then perhaps above all that she played a vital role in the moral welfare of her husband.

At the start of his second season at Newcastle, Alan wrecked his ankle in a pre-season tournament at Everton and for six months had to slowly fight his way back to fitness.

He had similar lay-offs with knee injuries before then at Blackburn, and after that at Newcastle.

Sitting on the sofa at home with his leg in a plaster cast isn't Alan's idea of fun, and Lainya admits: "He hates being injured.

"Like most footballers, he just lived to play. So when they can't play, they get frustrated. And Alan got VERY frustrated.

"He didn't take it out on us, but it was very hard. Not least because we had the children, and you cannot be down for long when you've got children around.

"So I had to help to lift his spirits. But that was only part of it, for Alan has great mental strength and my part was simply to add to that, to give something more to what was already there.

"He pulled himself through as much as anything, but I was there for him, and I think I played an important part."

SO WHAT COMES NEXT?

When Alan Shearer waves his farewells to the packed house at tonight's testimonial, and vanishes down the St. James' Park tunnel for the final time, his mind will turn again to what lies ahead. What has gone in the past will become only memories.

Many a good observer believes that the Shearer path will eventually lead to football management, and Lainya for her part, knowing its probable inevitability, will happily accept whatever comes along.

But in terms of the family, she sees another initial priority for her husband as he becomes an ex-footballer.

However, she is equally certain the pull of football will draw him back into the game before long.

She says: "I think he now needs to chill and spend quality time with the kids. They are still at an age where they can have that, and get a great deal from it.

"Alan has been in football ever since he left school, which means in all that time we have had only one holiday a year – and even for that, we had to take the children out of school.

"When he played for England, every other summer was taken up with tournaments, and when he retired from international football in 2000 family considerations were part of what he had in his mind.

"Football is a great life, and well-paid, don[t] get me wrong. There is never a time when I don't think we've been very lucky.

"But for most of the year we don't have weekends off. The amount of family wedding and christenings and other occasions I go to my own because Alan is playing or somethin[g] is the other side of being married to a footballer. The game brings many rewards, b[ut] there is a down side.

"We are really family-orientated, but it isn[t] always easy for the family. I think in all Alan'[s] time at Newcastle, we have only had Christm[as] Day together as a family twice.

"At three o'clock on Christmas afternoon, [Alan] has had to leave to join up with the team, an[d] while the children have never known any different, it isn't what any family would ideall[y] want. But we have accepted it as being part o[f] footballer's life.

"Even this year, our wedding anniversary i[s] on June 8th, and Alan will be covering the World Cup in Germany for television, which starts the following day.

"He wants to play more golf, and to spend quality time with the family, and in order to d[o] all that he needs to be free.

"But football is in his blood, and I would gi[ve] him six months at the most before he is champing at the bit to be back in football.

"And then he has to do what he has to do."

ALAN SHEARER OBE

PLUS FREEDOM OF THE CITY

2001 WAS A VERY GOOD YEAR

The year 2001 proved a real winner for Alan Shearer – in the civic field rather than on the football field. For in March he was awarded the Freedom of the City of Newcastle – a fitting tribute to one of the finest Geordies of them all (bottom picture).

And just three months later Alan and his family were guests at the Palace as he received the OBE (top) for services to the game.

GRAHAM TAYLOR, the England manager who handed Alan Shearer his national team debut, explains what made him an England idol.

I remember not so long ago having a conversation with Alan, and we talked about the time I handed him his England debut against France back in 1992.

Time certainly seems to have flown by since then, and when people say you should enjoy these types of moments, they are right. Because they quickly pass by.

I remember Alan back then. He was playing for Southampton at the time and from the moment he walked into the England set-up it was obvious we had something special on our hands.

He had this steely determination in his eyes, and that determination is still there to this day. There was an obvious determination to succeed.

Alan has a natural ability to hit the target. He may not always score, but if he doesn't then it's likely he will force the goalkeeper into a save.

I noticed quite quickly when I was working with Alan that he kept his head straight when he was shooting. If a golfer moves his head all over the place, the ball will go all over the place – and it's the same with a striker.

He was focused, he was still, he concentrated – and more often than not, he scored.

His game has changed over the years, as it does with all players. He used to work the channels like an old inside-right, and whip crosses into the box for his team-mates.

As time went on, he didn't do that as much, which is quite natural, but the one thing that hasn't changed throughout his career is that knack of putting the ball in the net. He has scored goals no matter what shirt he has been wearing.

As a manager, you tend to keep an eye on the players you give a debut to, and I have done that with Alan. It hasn't been too hard, mind you, because he hasn't had a bad career, has he!

Even if he hadn't managed to break Jackie Milburn record at St. James' Park, he'd still have been a legend on Tyneside - a living legend.

It goes without saying that I wish Alan all the very best on his big night.

THREE ENGLAND MANAGERS who had the benefit of a rampant Alan Shearer in their side tell what made him a world star.

Shearer's England

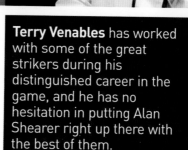

When **Glenn Hoddle** replaced Terry Venables as England boss in 1996, he had no hesitation in naming Alan Shearer as his captain...

"I had met Alan before I became England manager, and I knew he was a leader.

"You need that at international level, and the fact he was a striker may have raised a few eyebrows when I made my choice, but I had no hesitation.

"It is an old-fashioned view that a captain has to be someone at the back, someone who can see everything going on in front of them, but I didn't subscribe to that.

"I wanted someone who referees knew and respected, I wanted a main man to be my captain – and he was my main man.

"I also felt it was important at international level to have some continuity, it was no good having the captain changing every other game.

"Alan was always going to be the first name on my team sheet, so he was an obvious choice for me.

"Alan was like an extension of a manager, he took things out onto the pitch over that white line.

"He was tactically aware, he commanded respect from everyone in the dressing-room, particularly the younger lads at the time, but at the same time he wasn't the big 'I am' with the experienced players like Tony Adams or Paul Ince.

"Alan Shearer was the figurehead of that team, and he was a pleasure to work with.

"He was a great professional, he took immense pride in his training, never mind the matches, and he was a great role model.

"His record puts him up there with the likes of Jimmy Greaves, and he's without doubt the best I've worked with.

"Obviously the injury he picked up towards the end of the season brought a premature end for him, but as strange as it sounds, I believe that injury will tell him that the time was right to call it a day.

"Imagine if he scored a hat-trick on the last day of the season? He'd walk away wondering if he could go on for another season, if he'd be able to cut it come August after pre-season. That seed of doubt would have been there.

"He won't feel like that right now, but in the long run I think he'll look back and say the time was right. He won't be away long anyway, he just loves the game too much to walk away for good. He'll enjoy his break, but I've no doubts whatsoever he'll be back.

"Finally, I'd just like to wish him all the very, very best for his testimonial this evening.

"It is a marvellous gesture to donate the funds to charity, and at a time when football in general is a poor industry in terms of kicking itself, I applaud him for that.

"But I must add that it doesn't really surprise me.

"All the best Alan, enjoy the night – you deserve it."

Terry Venables has worked with some of the great strikers during his distinguished career in the game, and he has no hesitation in putting Alan Shearer right up there with the best of them.

"I was in charge of England for two years, and Alan played a key role in Euro 96, which was the major championship during my spell in charge.

"He had a lot of pressure on him going into that tournament, because he had gone through a barren spell of about 11 or 12 games without a goal.

"But he has this self-belief, and that stood him in good stead. There were a lot of strikers around at that time, lads like Robbie Fowler and Les Ferdinand were putting pressure on Alan and Teddy Sheringham, but it never entered my head to leave Alan out. Not once.

"He had a belief in himself, and I knew the only person who could stop that run was Alan. As long as he continued to believe in himself, the goals would come.

"And they did. He scored in the first game of Euro 96 against Switzerland, he then got one against Scotland followed by two against Holland.

"The Spain game ended goalless before we went through on penalties, and then in the semi-final he scored early on against Germany.

"He ended up as the top scorer in the tournament, and no-one mentioned the goal drought any more.

"He and Teddy made a great partnership, they were almost telepathic and they both knew the right time to shoot or pass.

"Alan was an out-and-out goalscorer, and the philosophy was simple – give him the ball, and he will score goals.

"He would get the poacher's goals, the six-yard tap-ins, but he'd also get the headers at the front post and the back post, the 30-yard screamers, the lot.

"He just loved scoring goals.

"I have worked with some of the game's greatest strikers over the years, and I would put Alan Shearer right up there with them.

"I feel privileged to have worked with him, and I wish him all the luck in the world both tonight and in whatever he chooses to do afterwards."

"One of the great strikers of his generation"

Gary Lineker played just three times with Alan Shearer for England, with the Geordie bursting onto the international stage towards the end of Lineker's own glittering career.

But Gary told Ian Willis how much he is looking forward to renewing his partnership with Alan in the Match of the Day studios next season...

England boss Sven Goran Eriksson pays tribute to Alan Shearer – and wishes he had the chance to work with the Magpies Number 9 on the international stage...

"I remember when Alan linked up with England back in 1992. He was a fresh-faced Geordie then, though he's still a fresh-faced Geordie now so things haven't changed really!" said Gary.

"It was obvious back then that he was a special talent, you could see that from the moment he walked into the first training session.

"He had something about him, he had strength and a good technique. He also had a bit of character, which has stayed with him all the way through his career.

"The first time we played together was against France at Wembley. Graham Taylor wanted to have a look at him, and I was on the bench that night. Alan scored, and I came on at half-time and got the other goal in a 2-0 win.

"We only played together a couple of times after that, which was a shame. I was coming to the end of my international career, and after the Euros in 1992 that was it for me.

"I'd like to think we could have struck up a decent partnership at international level, because on the couple of occasions we did link up, we dovetailed quite well.

"It would have been nice had I been a bit younger – or Alan a bit older – to see how we would have got on.

"Since then, obviously I have watched his career develop, as we all have.

"He is one of the great strikers of his generation, and his record is remarkable, it speaks for itself.

"He isn't just a goal-poacher, he has a bit of everything. He is an all-round target man, one of the best there has been."

Adds Gary: "In a way, I see a lot of similarities between my career and the one Alan has enjoyed.

"He may not have the trophies that he could have won had he signed for another club, but you cannot always judge a player by his medals.

"There are a lot of average players who can win a load of trophies in a great side, and sometimes the great players don't win as much in terms of silverware.

"But Alan wouldn't change that, and it speaks volumes for the man that he has spent so long with his home-town club."

Adds Gary: "I spent time up there when we filmed the documentary for my old England boss, Sir Bobby Robson, and even walking around the club and the training ground then, you could see that Alan had an aura about him with the people up in Newcastle.

"That aura, or presence, if you like, comes when people know what a person has achieved in their life, and that is the case with Alan Shearer."

While Alan has been lethal on the pitch over the years, Gary feels he has shown signs that he is going to be a major success off the field when he links up with the BBC team for Match of the Day.

Gary added: "He has the makings of being a top pundit, or an analyst, call it what you will.

"It's often a lot easier when you have finished playing, but to be fair to Alan he is straight-talking now and doesn't mind what he says, even if it is about his own team.

"He is blatantly honest, and we're very fortunate to have him with us on Match of the Day. I'm sure he will be a great addition to our team.

"The only thing he'll have to sort out is his clothing. To be fair to him he's been quite conservative with us on the BBC, but I remember a couple of his suits on Sky were a bit loud for him. Hopefully they will stay in the wardrobe now!"

"An occasion like this is fully deserved, I'm sure it will be a memorable evening that is fitting for Alan Shearer.

"I genuinely wish him well for the future."

"Alan Shearer had retired from the England team before I took over, but it would have been great for me to have had the opportunity to work with him.

"On more than one occasion, there were stories that Alan may reconsider his decision to finish playing international football, but they came to nothing.

"That was a shame for me, and also for the England team, because there was no doubt that Alan Shearer would have benefited any team.

"But I do believe that Alan's decision has benefited his club, and the fact he has gone on to break the records at Newcastle United backs that up.

"Even though I have not worked with Alan, I have watched his career closely.

"I remember some of his goals for Blackburn, I remember the goals he scored for England in Euro 96 and in the World Cup in France, and I have watched him score countless goals for Newcastle United.

"It is hard for anyone not to admire Alan Shearer.

"He is a tremendous ambassador for the game of football. He is admired by his fellow professionals, and if any young player wants a role model or someone to learn from, then look no further than Alan Shearer.

"He deserves praise for everything he has done for our game, for the country he played for and for all of the clubs he represented.

"He will be a miss to all of us, because he was one of the best."

Shearer's England

Alan Shearer was a throwback, the classic No 9, fearless and prolific.
He's the spirit of English football personified.
Only centre-halves will rejoice at his retirement.

Paul Hayward

He was a one off, the type of player school boys dream about becoming. A hero who wore No. 9 and scored goals no one else could. He has always been a model on and off the field for youngsters and arguably one of my best ever signings.

Lawrie McMenemy

At the final reckoning, the stats scream Shearer's class: yet it is words such as loyalty and devotion and not the impressive numbers, that truly define this special individual

Henry Winter

The only roots he has lost are those from his hair! People can see he's been a special player but equally he is as special as a person

Kenny Dalglish

What a pleasure it was to manage Alan during part of his England career and to be involved at a time when he achieved the ultimate accolade for a striker of being top goal scorer in Euro 96. He was my captain and away from the game I always think of him as a genuine individual and as a friend to me."

Terry Venables

Question.
What has always been and will always be the most important thing in football?
Answer. Putting the ball in the net.
Question. Who was the best at that?
Answer. Alan Shearer. **End of discussion !**

Graham Taylor

The perfect professional, the ultimate goal-scorer, the most respected footballer of a generation, a true ambassador for all that's positive in our game… undoubtedly, English football will be poorer for his absence.

Paul McCarthy

96 **appearances** 409 **goals** one **love**

THE GALLOWGATE ENDER ...

As a boy, Alan Shearer stood on the open terrace of the Gallowgate End watching United play in the Keegan era of the early 1980s.

So it was apt that two landmark goals in his career should be scored at that end of St. James' Park,

In the FA Cup-tie against Mansfield Town at St. James' on Saturday January 7th, scarcely 10 minutes remained when Albert Luque backheeled a Nobby Solano ball into the box and Shearer pounced to drive an unerring shot inside the left upright and equal Jackie Milburn's half-century-old 200-goal scoring record for the club.

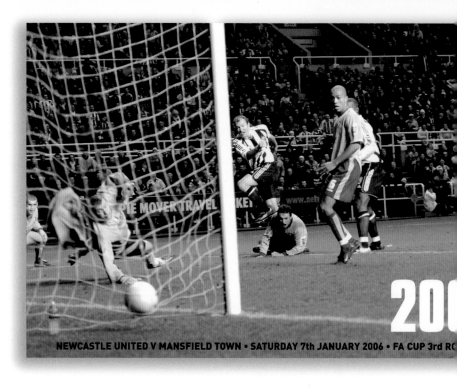

NEWCASTLE UNITED V MANSFIELD TOWN • SATURDAY 7th JANUARY 2006 • FA CUP 3rd RO

ALAN SHEARER
THE RECORD-BREAKER

NEWCASTLE UNITED V PORTSMOUTH • SATURDAY 4th FEBRUARY 2006 • BARCLAYS PREMIER

SHEARER BREAKS 50-YEAR JACKIE MILBURN GOALS RECORD ...

Four weeks later, on Saturday February 4th, Goal No. 201 arrived ... also at the Gallowgate End ...
United were leading Portsmouth in the Premiership by a single goal as the match moved into its 64th minute.

Shearer headed a ball to Shola Ameobi, ran on, and when Shola backheeled the ball perfectly into his path, raced away chased by Andy O'Brien to shoot past keeper Dean Kiely.

The prolonged ovation which greeted the goal gave Alan what he admits was one of the greatest feelings of his life. And for all those fortunate enough to witness it, **this was a moment to treasure forever.**

When Alan Shearer scored his record-setting 201st goal for Newcastle United against Portsmouth at St. James' Park on Saturday February 4th, 2006, the Geordie Nation celebrated a new landmark in the club's proud history.

But there was poignancy, too, as the near-50-year goals record of the great Jackie Milburn had finally been overtaken.

Ashington-born for Jackie scored the 200th and last of his 200 Newcastle goals at Chelsea on April 2nd, 1957, and between then and 2006 a succession of centre-forwards tried but failed to match his standards.

Finally, Shearer did it ... and as the new club record-holder receives his testimonial match at St. James' Park this evening, Jackie's widow Laura and son Jack pay their own personal tributes to the man who surpassed one of Tyneside's eternal heroes.

WELL DONE, ALAN ... IT REMINDED ME OF JACK

I will always remember the look of pure joy on Alan's face as the ball hit the back of the net for his 201st goal. I only saw it on TV but can just imagine what the atmosphere must have been like in the ground.

I did shed a few tears, though not because the long-standing record had been broken, simply because it brought back such lovely memories of Jack.

What seemed so nice to me was the modesty Alan displayed as he received the well-deserved accolades from the public and the media.

He appeared to be almost humbled by his achievement, very much in the way that Jack reacted after he surpassed Hughie Gallacher's record. In that way, I think they are very similar.

It was also lovely to hear the kind words he had for Jack.

Well done, Alan ... thoroughly well deserved.

LAURA MILBURN

MILBURN

LIKE JACK, ALAN WON THE HEARTS OF THE GEORDIE NATION

People often ask me to compare Alan's style of play to my own father's, but to be honest, it is very difficult. Two prolific goalscorers, yes, but two quite different types of player.

The '50s game is poles apart compared to modern-day and I have no doubt that in another 50 years it will have changed just as much again.

Back in the old days, memories are of heavy boots, burdensome cotton shirts and shorts and a sopping wet leather ball, though we must remember too the deep muddy pitches on which they had to display their talents.

I reckon that few of today's lightweight, albeit fitter, players would have made much of an impact back then, with the definite exception of one.

Alan Shearer. With his bustling power, he would have breezed it, even after an eight-hour shift down the pit followed by a bus ride to St. James' Park. I'm quite sure that Alan could adapt to any playing situation.

So, how would my father cope today with the lightweight gear and ball? I think he would manage very nicely, though without a doubt he would have to give up the fags.

However, there is something that I do have great difficulty picturing him doing and that is driving back home to Ashington in a Ferrari!

When Alan cracked the record, and had my father been watching from above, I just know that he would have been willing his fellow-Geordie on.

And even though Alan didn't manage to bag a trophy during his time at the club, he won the most important thing ... he won the hearts of the Geordie nation.

JACK MILBURN

SHEARER

He's Simply The Best

"The best British-style centre-forward we have ever had."

That is the glowing assessment of Alan Shearer from one of Newcastle United's finest servants, and one of Alan's closest friends, **ROB LEE**.

Rob was at Newcastle for four years before Shearer arrived, and had become an adopted Geordie by the time a real one walked into St. James' Park with a £15m price tag hanging from his Number Nine shirt in the summer of 1996.

And the man whose job it was to feed the goal machine with chances says: "You always knew with Alan that if you got balls to him in the box, he would guarantee that they would end up in the net.

"At 35 he was still the best target man in the game, even if he had lost a little of the pace he had 10 years ago. After all, we all had pace 10 years ago!

"He scored goals, he held the ball up, he brought people in, he won headers, he put great crosses in – he had the lot, and nine times out of 10 whatever he tried came off.

"Being a centre-forward, he knew when he went wide what sort of ball a striker liked – and so he would whip it in as good as any winger. It's only a pity he couldn't be on the end of his own crosses!

"I got my goal in the FA Cup semi-final at Wembley against Chelsea in 2000 from one of Al's crosses – and he's never stopped reminding me of it!

"He also set up my first goal for England, which was special. Mind you, he owed me a few for all the ones I served up for him over the years!!"

When United wrote the world's biggest football transfer cheque in July 1996 to bring Shearer home from Blackburn Rovers it was in a bid to complete the Premier League Championship jigsaw that had come so close to finality under manager Kevin Keegan.

And like all of the United players who flew to the Far East in the 1996-97 pre-season, Rob remembers Keegan alighting from the plane to seal the Shearer transfer while the rest of the party was fastening their seatbelts.

"Yes, we did think Alan was the last piece of the jigsaw," Rob says. "When Kevin got off the plane, we knew it was going to be a major signing.

"But we thought: 'Blimey, how can we improve this team?' – then when we discovered it was Alan, that answered our question."

Alan and Les Ferdinand shared 49 goals between them as United finished runners-up for the second successive year in 1996-97, and Rob says: "Alan's partnership with Les was the best we've ever had. Every game they seemed to score in a team that was made to get goals. It really was a joy to play in. Every time we went out, no matter who we were playing, we believed we were going to win.

"Half-way through that 1996-97 season, though, Kevin left - and things changed. When Kevin left, we were still in a strong pos[ition] and still in the FA Cup, but we got put out of t[he] Cup although we did get into the Champions League by finishing second again.

"I honestly feel that the team we had at the start of season 1996-97, with Alan in it, was better than the team that finished 1995-96 – great as that team was.

"However, we had a difficult start to 1996-[97] because we'd been on the tiring Far East trip[,] then got a 4-0 beating off Manchester United [in] the Charity Shield, and it took us time toget[her] into it.

"But I still feel that that team was even be[tter] than the team which came so close to winnin[g] the Championship the year before."

Off the field, Rob and his wife Anna have become close friends of Alan and his wife Lainya. They often go out together socially, a[nd] Rob is one of the former players invited by A[lan] to play in his team against Celtic.

Says Rob, tongue-in-cheek: "Al is a typica[l] Geordie – he does tricks, he's mad, and he's good fun! He's also intelligent, because he on[ly] lets people see what he wants them to see.

"He has a laugh and a joke with his close friends, but he's got to be wary because he is such a big name with a big reputation.

"You can either be a big name who gets in the magazines and papers, or you can do wh[at] Al does and look after the family, which he do[es] very well.

"He has a circle of people he knows and trusts, he will look after them, and they will lo[ok] after him."

Adds Rob, who at the age of 40 is still play[ing] for Wycombe Wanderers: "Al's a top bloke, a[nd a] top player – and it will be an honour to take p[art] in his testimonial match.

"I'm looking forward to coming back – I sti[ll] miss the Newcastle people, and every time I come back I get on well with everyone.

"But tonight is all about Alan Shearer, and this is going to be a fantastic occasion for one of the best players the game has ever seen."

PEDRO

PETER BEARDSLEY and Alan Shearer have more than one thing in common. They're both Geordies, they're both top-class footballers, and they've both captained the home-town team they love, Newcastle United. As well as England.

Both men have enjoyed numerous peaks in the game but little can match leading the players down the tunnel at St. James' Park with a full-house Toon Army waiting to roar the side onto the field.

It's a feeling Beardsley has experienced numerous times, and he says: "Being captain of your home-town club is really special. It's an unbelievable feeling. And the great thing for me is that I'm one of the few in this part of the world who can realise and know what Al felt when he led the team out of the tunnel."

It's all about the particularly special pride that Geordies feel for their own, and Pete goes on: "You are the first to see the fans on the far side of the pitch, and in the spring months in particular it's all black-and-white over there. That's what you see, and it's very special, believe me."

Very special. They are exactly the words that can be applied to people like Alan Shearer and Peter Beardsley. And they're doubly special when they play in the same team together, as they did when Alan signed for United from Blackburn Rovers for £15m on the eve of the 1996-97 season.

Peter remembers the saga of the Shearer signing vividly – and recalls also how he had to act as insurance cover as the new recruit travelled across the Far East on his first mission for Newcastle United!

He says: "We were boarding the flight to head to the Far East, but then Kevin Keegan got off the plane and we knew it was the big one, though at that stage we didn't know it was Alan.

"A day or two later when it all came to fruition we were in the hotel and we saw it on TV in the hotel where it was massive news.

"The great thing for me was that Al came to Singapore and I got asked if I would fly from Singapore to Japan with him because he wasn't insured. So me and Al made the flight with the directors, and I got to know him on that flight.

"I remember Al saying how he wanted to come home, but he also knew it was going to be a fantastic team and he was going to be a major part of it.

"We finished second in 1996-97, as we had in 1995-96, but we had some incredible runs – the amount of games we went unbeaten was tremendous.

"The signing gave us a big buzz. The fact that he had turned down Manchester United, who were the champions, added to it, and the reception Al got from the fans was unbelievable."

On the pitch, the presence of Shearer and Les Ferdinand in the front line was a guaranteed goals supply line – and for the midfield men behind them it gave so many options in delivering the forward pass.

"They were always available for the ball," Beardsley says. "Al was always prepared to go into a wide position, and he was a great crosser of the ball.

"Whereas someone like Gary Lineker, who was a great player and goalscorer, was a penalty box player, Al was always prepared to go into areas other than the box.

"Without a doubt Al was one of the best – and it wasn't only about scoring goals, either. He made so many, too – altogether, I would think he must have been involved in about 400 or more.

"For England, myself and David Platt were the two behind Al, and he kicked on another level when Teddy Sheringham came into the team. They had great awareness and understanding and formed a top-class partnership, as you could see from so many of the goals they scored.

"Euro 96 was probably his best tournament, and the one Al enjoyed the most, with the game against Holland when Al got two in a 4-1 win particularly great for him. On that day he was involved in most of the things England did."

There were many, many memorable moments in that first season in which Shearer paraded his talents in a black-and-white shirt, and one of the most memorable of all came in October 1996 when champions Manchester United came to town on a day when both sides had something to prove.

Manchester United had snatched away the previous year's title but it was Newcastle who did all the proving as Alex Ferguson's team was systematically dismantled and destroyed to the tune of 5-0. Darren Peacock, David Ginola and Les Ferdinand all scored before Shearer hit Number Four.

"Al put the ball in after a couple of attempts had been saved," recalls Beardsley, "and the

way he wheeled away it was fantastic for him. I'll never forget the look of delight on his face that day when he scored that goal.

"The two semi-finals, when Al scored once against Sheffield United and twice against Tottenham, were really special too.

"I was there for both of those and the stand on the far side at Old Trafford was literally bouncing. They were both wonderful occasions for everyone."

Shearer's style of captaincy, says Beardsley, was always to lead by example. And it was some example.

"Leading by example is something he has always done. He is not an aggressive shouter, but he does it by example. He knows when to tackle and when to get the crowd going and he can make the game come alive.

"He plays it the old-fashioned way, and isn't afraid to make a physical challenge, but the good thing about him is that when he then shakes your hand at the end of the game he looks into your eyes with respect. He knows the value of respect.

"The Newcastle United goalscoring record is a brilliant achievement. I never saw Jackie Milburn play but obviously he was a special player, yet to do what Al has done in the modern game, when a lot more happens, is something else."

Beardsley has played with many of the game's leading strikers and rather than select his best-ever, he selects three players as the greatest strikers he has had the honour of playing with.

Alan Shearer's name, inevitably, is up there. So is that of former United star Andy Cole. And so is Beardsley's England partner Gary Lineker.

"Al would be in the top three of all those that I've ever played with," Peter says, "with Coley and Gary Lineker up there too, and not particularly putting one ahead of the others. They have all been great strikers, with their own individual characteristics."

BRYANADAMS

FOR ONE NIGHT ONLY

LIVE

AT ST. JAMES' PARK

NEWCASTLE UNITED FOOTBALL CLUB

6 JUNE 2006
DOORS OPEN 5PM

NEWCASTLE UNITED

IN ASSOCIATION WITH

SQUARELEG
ENTERTAINMENT

NUFC BOX OFFICE **0191 2611 571** (OFFICE HOURS)   WWW.NUFC.CO.UK

SEE TICKETS **0870 1660 441** (24HR)   WWW.SEETICKETS.COM

TICKETMASTER **0870 6077 416** (24HR)   WWW.TICKETMASTER.CO.UK

HOSPITALITY PACKAGES AVAILABLE – PLEASE CALL 0191 2018 719 FOR FURTHER DETAILS

DAVID HARRISON
CHIEF SPORTS WRITER, NEWS OF THE WORLD

David Harrison has followed the career of Alan Shearer closely over the years ghost-writing some of Alan's books as well as his regular News of the World column.

Let me tell you about the Alan Shearer I know. Well, actually, there are two of them.

One is the serious, stern-faced, rather sullen character you often see on your television screens, offering diplomatic verdicts and sidestepping controversy.

Not quite Mary Poppins but certainly shades of Julie Andrews with huge dollops of sugar to help the medicine go down.

Alan adopted this persona at the start of his illustrious career, presumably with the idea of projecting a wholesome image that would endear him to the public at large and, coincidentally, the commercial moguls who wanted him to endorse their products.

It worked to such an extent that Alan's former England team-mate Tim Flowers often referred to him as Mr Mogadon. Or sometimes it was Billy Big Pockets as an acknowledgment to the wealth he accrued from his clubs and sponsors.

I ghosted Alan's newspaper columns and three books with him over the course of six years and rarely did he divert from the script when we were "on the record".

But there is another Alan Shearer behind the mask. This one is a mischievous, fun-loving rascal who can be the heart and soul of any dressing room – a man's man in every sense. He is single-minded, bloody-minded, self-opinioned and loves an argument – as long as he wins it.

But the private face of Alan can also be kind and caring. I have lost count of the number of favours he has done for me and he will not thank me for mentioning the endless hours he devotes to charitable causes without seeking reward or publicity.

Since the year 2000 there have been two loves in Alan's life – Newcastle United and his family. To serve them he gave up his international career.

But his country's loss has been Newcastle's gain. And that brings me to yet another image of Shearer, the one you all know so well, smashing in a brilliant goal and turning with one arm raised to celebrate in front of his devoted public.

I was watching some old videos of Alan the other day and there was one goal that summed him up perfectly. He shrugged off a strong challenge from Gary Pallister, and left the Manchester United defender clutching his throat and gasping for breath before slamming home a left foot shoot.

Sadly, we won't be seeing any more of that after this season but I am sure the memories will live on with all those who witnessed his record-breaking deeds.

I shall remember him as a fantastic footballer and a formidable person and I am proud to know him as a friend.

And now I stand by for a bucket-load of abuse from him for offering such gushing praise.

MARTIN TYLER
SKY SPORTS

MY PREMIERSHIP TOP 3:
1. Shearer
2. Shearer
3. Shearer

Wherever I go, people come up to me and ask me to shout "SHEARER!" as I do when describing his goals in my commentary. It's become something of a trademark for me, but I have lost count of the times I have had to say it because Alan has scored so many goals when I've been lucky enough to have been holding the microphone.

I would say, without doubt, that he is the best player there has ever been in the Premiership. My top three would be Alan Shearer at number one, Alan Shearer at number two, and Alan Shearer at number three.

When you look at his record over the various seasons, and take into account the injuries he has had, it is phenomenal. I recall he once put off an operation so he could reach the landmark of scoring 30 or more goals in three successive seasons!

I remember him bursting onto the scene at Southampton. I remember the goals he scored at Crystal Palace on the opening day of the season when he made his debut for Blackburn all those years ago. I remember him being the driving force behind Blackburn's Championship win, which came on that unforgettable day at Anfield.

I've seen countless goals for his beloved Newcastle United – what a feeling that must be to score for those fans in the Gallowgate End wearing the Number 9 shirt – and he's done the same for his country.

Alan Shearer is a wonderful craftsman, and is a fine example not just to a footballer, but to anyone in any walk of life.

I have a son of my own, and I wonder how he would have coped if he had left home just as Alan did years ago and travelled to the opposite end of the country to pursue his career.

He obviously had the same single-mindedness and determination to succeed back then as he has to this day.

I have had the pleasure of working with Alan in commentary, and he prepares for a match as though he is playing in it. He'll go through the stats, look at the players, and discuss any issues that may come up in the game.

I'm sure he will be a success as a manager one day, but he has already shown to me that he will be successful in the broadcasting world as well.

We'll have to see what the future holds for Alan, but I remember when he made his decision to join the BBC and Match of the Day. He contacted a lot of the people who he had worked with at Sky Sports – myself included – and explained his decision and the reasons behind it.

That is a measure of the man. It simply enhanced my respect for him and I wish him every success in whatever he chooses to do when he hangs up his boots.

I am certain tonight will prove to be a fantastic occasion, and fitting for the man it is arranged for.

All the best Alan – I hope you go out there tonight and score 10!

MICK LOWES
BBC RADIO NEWCASTLE

Some years ago, I was privileged and honoured to work with one of the greatest footballers of all time.

Whether at home or abroad, when covering the World Cup finals in Italy in 1990, I never ceased to be amazed by the attitude and dignity of one of the game's greatest names.

Whether Princes or Paupers, everyone was treated equally, no-one more important than the next.

The greatest compliment I can pay Alan Shearer is that he and the late, great Bobby Moore could have been peas in a pod - two of a kind.

Working with Alan over the past decade, particularly on public phone-ins and talk-ins, I've seen first-hand that same human touch.

Like his predecessor as England captain, it's clear that home is where the heart is and that working-class roots would never be severed at any price.

You can take the boy out of Newcastle, but you can never take Tyneside out of its greatest-ever goalscorer.

Humility and greatness are rarely found side by side in any human being, but Alan Shearer and Bobby Moore have – and had – it by the bucketful.

Have a great night, Alan.

SHEAR LEGEND

Alan Shearer Tribute Supplement

DON'T MISS YOUR

Evening **Chronicle**

BIG NEWS • BIG VALUE • BIG HEART

Friday, 12th May 2006

Made in Tyneside. *For you.*

In the Summer of '96

CHIEF SPORTSWRITER OF THE EVENING CHRONICLE ALAN OLIVER RECALLS THE START OF THE TOON SHEARER-ERA

I was lucky enough to be in Bangkok when Newcastle United announced the £15m signing of Alan Shearer.

And I am lucky enough to be here at St. James' Park tonight when Alan Shearer plays his last game in a black and white shirt.

And do you know what? The bit in between hasn't been bad either.

In fact I would also say that I have been extremely lucky to have seen Alan Shearer's 10-year stint as not only player, but also main goalscorer, captain, talisman and ambassador of Newcastle United.

Looking back to the summer of 1996, United fans were down in the dumps after they had seen their side caught by Alex Ferguson's Manchester United in the previous season in the search for their first premiership championship success.

And if they could have chosen one player on the planet – yes, on the planet - to bring to St. James' Park then that player would have been one of their own.

The sheet metalworker's son from Gosforth. Alan Shearer.

That's what Shearer meant to the fans of Newcastle United.

From the moment he arrived he has never let them down. And it has not been his fault that a major trophy has eluded Newcastle.

After the announcement of the signing in Bangkok I can remember Big Al flying out to Singapore with club photographer Ian Horrocks and I bumped into him in the gym at the Traders Hotel.

He managed to say a quick "nice to meet you" before I was unceremoniously shuffled away by the hotel security even though I was a fellow-guest and perfectly entitled to be there.

I didn't like to tell him that we had already met. In those days, unlike now, I was a bit fashion-conscious and while it was the butt of many jokes from Kevin Keegan I was proud of my green jacket.

But I must have looked like one of the stewards. Because one night when Blackburn were playing at St. James' Park, Shearer left the players' lounge and I thought I would nip in for a quick interview but I was stopped in my tracks when he asked me if his taxi had arrived.

And to tell the truth while I have met some of the biggest names in the game I have always been a bit in awe of Big Al and I didn't have the heart to tell him I wasn't a steward.

However, what he will not need telling is what an honour it has been watching him banging in the goals week in week out.

Yet one of my lasting memories has nothing to do with his amazing goal tally. It came not too long ago when United beat Aston Villa at Villa Park in February.

If you remember, United, 2-1 up, were hanging on with 10 men after Celestine Babayaro had been sent off.

Shearer was literally playing on one leg because of a calf injury and he missed the next few games.

But twice in the last five minutes he took the ball into the left-hand corner and despite the howls of frustration from the Villa fans and the efforts of the home players - not all of them legal – they couldn't do a thing with him. There wasn't any glory in this for Alan Shearer but for me it just sums up what playing for Newcastle United has meant to him.

We're going to miss you, Al.

Project **Brazil**

7 - 16 October 2006

BOBBY MOORE FUND

CANCER RESEARCH UK

Join the Bobby Moore Fund for Cancer Research UK on a ten day project in Brazil – a once in a lifetime experience to renovate a remote Brazilian school, build a football pitch and play football against an official Brazilian team. All sponsorship money raised will help the Bobby Moore Fund to tackle bowel cancer through vital research.

www.bobbymoorefund.org   0870 850 8735

Registered charity no.1089464

HENRY WINTER
THE DAILY TELEGRAPH

SHEARER ...
THE PATRIOTIC
PREDATOR

WHEN all the doubters ganged up on Alan before Euro 96, when his England goal drought stretched back 20 months, I occasionally saw him in the Wembley car park after all those warm-up games against Hungary, Portugal, and Colombia.

Alan was making his way slowly to his car, his body battered by the evening's combat. His ankles had been kicked black and blue, elbows had been flicked into his face and he had run everywhere.

Alan's body was battered, but his belief wasn't. This great England No 9 knew he would deliver when it counted.

After meeting Alan's father one day at Wembley, I understood more about Alan the competitor. Never complain. Never stop working. Take the hits. Take the criticism. Give everything, an honest shift of work, and reward will come your way. A defender's slip, a half-chance, a glimpse of goal. It will come.

The FA's archives contain many photographs but few more dramatic than the moment against the Swiss when Alan catches the ball, pouring all his energy and determination into the shot. The picture I love most captures Alan side-on: his left foot, studs rooted in the Wembley turf, steadies his body while the right boot, swinging into the ball powerfully, does the real damage. The ball rose violently into the roof of the net, and England had lift-off.

The sun shone on Wembley that memorable summer, and particularly on Alan. He was brilliant, the model of the modern-day centre-forward, all good touch and endless running. Against Scotland, Alan rose to meet a Gary Neville cross, giving poor Andy Goram no chance.

Next up were the Dutch, a class act with players like Dennis Bergkamp in their pomp, but they were routed 4-1 with Shearer striking like lightning – twice. The second, a first-time finish from Teddy Sheringham's disguised pass, still illuminates the memory of all privileged to be present.

Football was coming home in style.

And so to the knock-out stages, to a penalty in the successful shoot-out against Spain and then that fourth-minute header against Germany in the semi-finals.

No winner's medal came Alan's way at Euro 96, but he finished leading scorer. Alan also secured the respect of everyone on the England scene, from players who marvelled at his hunger and goals, from fans who loved a patriotic predator, and from those of us hacks who enjoyed his honest observations, even when one of the arch-wags of the England dressing-room formed sound-bites at France 98 out of Abba song titles. We met our Waterloo with Alan.

Of the millions of deserved compliments that will be paid to Alan during his testimonial perhaps the greatest is this: he never let his country down.

JOHN GIBSON
EVENING CHRONICLE

WE ALL HAVE OUR
OWN SPECIAL
MEMORIES OF ALAN
SHEARER

SOME men are destined to stand apart. Heroes who become legends and are thus secured in history for life and beyond.

Alan Shearer has achieved such lofty status. Newcastle United's record goalscorer, captain of club and country. A No.9 legend in a Geordie land where that counts for everything.

Shearer of course smashed the record of another such No.9, Jackie Milburn, this season. It's been my pleasure to know both of them and they are special, as men as well as footballers.

This evening the final curtain drops on a distinguished career, that of the greatest centre-forward in Premier League history.

Shearer is the Magpie who thieved goals for 10 years, topping 200 of them - the teak-tough leader whose power of boot and head destroyed all those who attempted to stand in his way.

Alan operated in the minefield that is the penalty area, a back alley of flick-knives and muggings rather than long-distance cannon fire. He prowled where in-fighting abounded and flourished rather than died.

His was the most pressurised of jobs, a place where there is no hiding but plenty of glory for the brave. And that he was, a centre-forward who gave as much stick as he took, who fought over every blade of grass. Defenders couldn't bully Shearer.

We'll all take away our special memories of a special player. Mine will be his wondrous goal here against Everton, his strikes which won FA Cup semi-finals in successive seasons, his five-goal haul against Sheffield Wednesday, and for sheer drama and dripping emotion the goal that provided him with Newcastle's record in the victory over Portsmouth.

However, I'll remember much more. The serious guy in public who is tremendous fun away from the cameras, the kind man who gave his services free and filled to bursting-point a vast room in St. James' Park to do a chat show and raise money to save my club Gateshead in our hour of need.

He is loyal – ask Jack Hixon, the scout who put him on the road to fame – but doesn't tolerate fools, which is fine. He expects to be treated as he would treat you and providing he is there's no problem.

May retirement shine sweetly upon him. It is thoroughly deserved. Alan Shearer has shared a glittering career with thousands of fellow-Geordies and has been our standard-bearer over the last decade and beyond, when he was at Southampton and Blackburn Rovers.

Let the trumpets blare and the drums roll in his honour.

BOB CASS
MAIL ON SUNDAY

HE would be the last person to admit it but Alan Shearer's paucity of football honours is purely and simply the result of his passionate devotion to his roots.

Loyalty comes easy to kids born into families who support Manchester United, Liverpool or Arsenal.

Chelsea's more recent heavily-subsidised successes will no doubt attract a new age of schoolboy hopefuls to Stamford Bridge ... but the opportunity to win a league championship or even a European Cup medal has never been the kind of lure behind the urge to wear black and white stripes.

Like the famous local beer, the number nine shirt was the one Shearer was always going to come back for.

History might not have been his bang at school but he was brought up on the folklore associated with legendary strikers such as Jackie Milburn and Malcolm Macdonald. His classroom dreams were all about being their kind of local hero.

The fact that his route back was via Southampton and then Blackburn Rovers was due firstly to a lack of judgement on Newcastle's part and secondly to their lack of cash as well as ambition ... factors that, to anyone even minutely less committed to his destiny, might just have put him off for good.

And there were even greater temptations - none greater than the chance to become part of a Manchester United side that went on to win eight league titles, four FA Cups, one League Cup and, oh yes, the European Cup.

I remember back in the summer of 1992 when Sir Alex Ferguson desperately attempted to hijack Alan's move to Blackburn.

The Man U manager, knowing I was able to contact Shearer, called me to try and find out how far down the line the deal had gone. `Tell him he's too late,' was Shearer's reply ... a man of honour, he would not let his principles allow him to renege on the gentleman's agreement he had with Kenny Dalglish.

Four years and a title medal later he turned Sir Alex down again when his hometown club, now fired with overdue ambition and fortified by the financial backing of Sir John Hall, offered him a deal he did not want to refuse. The rest, as they say ...

Dispassionate neutrals have doubted Shearer's sanity. Why choose Newcastle in front of the biggest football club in the world?'

To be fair his answer would hardly convince anyone south of Tyneside that he wasn't a candidate for the funny farm.

"You have to be born as Geordie to realise what this club means to us. Newcastle United has always been everything to me."

Ask him to swap, as the club's highest-ever goalscorer, the realisation of that classroom dream for the honours he might have won elsewhere ... no contest!

So now the Toon Army will get to say `thanks' to one of their `ain'.

It promises to be one of football's biggest-ever send-offs ... and it still might not be enough.

THOSE FA CUP SEMI-FINALS...

The Ecstasy & The Agony

NEWCASTLE UNITED reached the Semi-Finals of the FA Cup four times in Alan Shearer's 10 years at the club.

Twice in a row, in 1998 and 1999, United emerged victorious as Alan first cracked in the winner against Sheffield United, then followed up with the two goals that sank Tottenham Hotspur.

Both of those Semi-Finals were staged at Old Trafford, which might not have been a lucky ground in the league for the Magpies, but was certainly a lucky one in the FA Cup.

However, when United went to their third successive semi-final, in 2000, they had to travel to Wembley to face Chelsea ... and lost.

It took another five years for the Magpies to make the last four again – and the 2005 clash with Manchester United at Cardiff was the most disappointing of the lot.

Alan Shearer played in all four matches ... and he recalls the agony and the ecstasy of the Semi-Final rollercoaster.

1998: BLUNTING THE BLADES

Alan had not yet recovered from the serious ankle injury sustained in pre-season at Everton by the time United launched their FA Cup bid in 1998.

United won – ironically at Everton – without him in Round Three, but he returned just in time for the fourth round tie away to non-league Stevenage Borough, scored the three goals that eliminated Stevenage after a replay, and figured in the home victories over Tranmere and Barnsley that led to the semi-final against Sheffield United.

A crowd of 53,000 packed Old Trafford, and Alan recalls: "Everyone expected us to beat Sheffield United, because they were in the First Division – but they gave us a hell of a good fight.

"It was never going to be an easy game, but they kept it tight even after falling behind to my goal in the second half had a real go for it. And we were pushed.

"I remember the atmosphere was sensational. My family told me that the big stand on the far side was physically moving with all the Newcastle fans celebrating in it. They could really feel it physically shaking.

"When I scored, the fans were going mad, and I made the most of it in front of them. If you can't milk that, then you can't milk anything.

"Sheffield United had a couple of half-chances which they didn't make the most of. Wayne Quinn, who later joined us, had at least one.

"But we prevailed in the end with a good cross from 'Digger' – John Barnes – to get the goal that won it.

"First of all I thought my header was going in, but the keeper saved it. The defender had gone onto the deck but I was still running onto it and my momentum was carrying me forward. I stood up on my feet and smashed it in from almost on the line.

"They then took the attitude that if they were going to get beaten they may as well go down with a fight, and they really went all out for an equaliser.

"We held on, but it certainly wasn't a comfortable victory. It was very, very tough."

1999: SINKING THE SPURS

"I think the experience of being there in 1998 helped us in 1999. It was the same ground, the fans were in the same place, and we knew what it was all about. Even the atmosphere was similar. It wasn't a re-run, exactly, but we knew what it was all about.

"It was a very even game, and a very tough one. In the second half of the 90 minutes Nikos Dabizas handled the ball in our box – it was one of those which I've seen given though it wasn't deliberate, but the ref didn't give it, and I guess you could say that in that respect we got away with it a bit. But we deserved it.

"It was ironic that in extra time we got a penalty for a very clear handball against Sol Campbell, when he reached up above his head to pull down a ball that was going over him.

"I remember feeling the pressure on that one because it was a big penalty in a big game and in front of our fans as well.

"The Spurs keeper was Ian Walker, who had trained with umpteen times with England and taken practice penalties again, again and again. So he would have reckoned he'd know my thoughts.

"I went to his left because I thought he thought that his right-hand side was my favourite side – and it worked. He went the wrong way.

"After that our tails were up and we were soaking up the atmosphere. The penalty came in the second half of extra time so we didn't have long to hold on, but we wanted a second goal to kill the game off.

"Then I got a ball and passed it to Silvio (Maric) and he got outside and pulled it back for me on the edge of the box. I caught it sweetly first-time with my right foot and it was one of those where you know you've hit it right and that it's going in.

"It flew across Walker and under the bar and it was 2-0 and that was it. All over. We were at Wembley for the Final again.

"And it felt absolutely great."

> **"I remember the atmosphere was sensational. My family told me that the big stand was physically moving with all the Newcastle fans celebrating in it"**

2000: CHOKED BY CHELSEA

"We played well at Wembley against Chelsea, but were out of luck and for the third year in a row we lost there in the FA Cup.

"We'd lost the 1998 Finals to Arsenal and Manchester United – who were going for the Double and Treble respectively – and I remember saying after the Chelsea game that they should knock the place down. And they did eventually!

"Gus Poyet was the man who did the damage – he scored both Chelsea goals, heading their winner after Rob Lee's equaliser.

"It was a great header from Rob that brought us level from my cross, but Poyet, who had scored a good few goals against us previously, haunted us again. We played as well as in the two semi-finals against Sheffield United and Tottenham, but I think it's fair to say that the opposition in 2000 was probably slightly better.

"It just went against us on the day, unfortunately. But although the game was played in London, I don't think that gave Chelsea any particular advantage. We still had all our fans there, as usual, and it was evens in that respect.

"They just got the goals on the day – but we gave a good account of ourselves."

2005: ROUTED BY THE RED DEVILS

"I have to admit we were well outlclassed by Manchester United at Cardiff last year. But our build-up to the game wasn't ideal.

"We'd gone to Lisbon to play Sporting in the UEFA Cup quarter-final on the Thursday three days before the game and lost 4-1, 4-2 on aggregate, after being ahead, but I think the disappointment of Lisbon was not the main factor in our poor performance at Cardiff.

"We had injured players out and suspended players out, and it was always going to be difficult against a class team that had had a far more comfortable build-up to the semi than us.

"I wouldn't honestly say we were tired after Lisbon. I don't think that was it. I just think we were beaten by a better team on the day.

"Their 11 was simply a better 11 than ours.

"We went 2-0 behind by half-time and were 3-0 down by the time Shola scored for us. But even when Shola scored to make it 3-1 I don't think we were in with any realistic chance. Just to make things worse, it was pouring down with rain and after being done in the quarter-final of the UEFA Cup, getting done again against Manchester United really put our season on the downward slope."

United physios Derek Wright and Paul Ferris have been at Newcastle United all the time Alan Shearer has been – and longer.

And Alan's injury record means they've had a big influence on his career – by getting him fit and back out on the pitch.

Alan has been their star patient all too often, and he says of the two 'phizzes': "Derek and Paul have been a very important part of my career at Newcastle United. Every time I've been injured, they've put me right and got me back playing again.

"No player could have had better treatment."

Says Derek: "Alan's a joy to work with because he does everything you ask."

And Paul agrees: "He self-motivates, and he's an honest and straightforward bloke."

Paul has never forgotten a personal touch from Alan that he says symbolises the man.

In America with Alan for 0 days while surgeon Richard Steadman worked on his injured knee, Paul didn't know his wife Geraldine had received a bouquet of flowers back home.

"And they were from Alan, with a note reading: 'Sorry for keeping your husband away from you'. That says a great deal about Alan Shearer. He cares about people."

And Paul adds: "That was several years ago, but the amazing thing is that the course of exercises Steadman gave Alan to do, he still does every single day – back, hamstring and so on.

"And there was another one, after the FA Cup-tie against Stevenage in 1998, at Alan got hammered in the press for not swapping shirts with the Stevenage centre-half in either the first game or the replay.

"But what people don't know is that he kept those shirts, framed them, and presented them to myself and Derek as his thanks for getting him through the first injury of all, the ruptured ankle and fractured fibula that he suffered pre-season at Everton six months and more before. And we've treasured them."

Derek says: "Alan's very sensible. When he's injured, he's so determined to get back as soon as possible that he tries to beat the record for any player getting back in such-and-such a time. But when it comes to playing again, he knows what he can do and only returns when he's absolutely ready."

"His determination is remarkable. When he got injured in his last game at Sunderland, it was obvious it was bad. I told him that he'd done his ligaments but he said he'd only come off if they'd snapped! In the end, he couldn't carry on – but he made every attempt to do so."

Both physios are agreed that Alan has all it takes to one day become a manager.

Paul says: "He's very insightful, and a good judge of character who knows how to be in charge of people."

And Derek agrees: "He certainly has what it takes to be a manager. I'm sure that one day he will come back into football."

The Physios

The men who kept Al together

THE SCHOOL REPORT: COULDN'T DO BETTER!

Alan Shearer hasn't been a net-bulging striker all his football life ... just ask Jimmy Nelson.

For Jimmy was Alan's school team manager at Gosforth High in the mid-1980s and admits he used his star player in the middle of the park because he could have a greater influence there.

Captain Al still scored a hatful of goals and became so valuable to Jimmy's Under-14, Under-15 and Under-16 teams that if he was ever off sick, the manager would try to get the game postponed!

"He was unquestionably the best player in the team," says Jimmy, who is now Head of Education and Welfare at the Newcastle United Academy. "But more often then I would play him in midfield because I needed him on the ball as much as possible.

"There was more chance of him getting the ball in midfield than there was of him getting it up front.

"He would make surging runs and still score loads of goals. In fact, I remember one match against John Marlay School when he got the ball on the edge his own box, set off – with me screaming at him all the way to lay it off – and finished by blasting it into the net from the edge of the other box. I told him off afterwards for not passing ..."

But he readily pays tribute to the factors that have made Shearer one of the biggest names in world football.

Jimmy says: "Hand on heart, if you'd asked me when Alan was 16 if he would become one of the greatest centre-forwards in the world, I would have said No. And I would have been wrong.

"I always thought he had a great chance of making it in the game, but didn't think he would develop the way he has, and reach the very top."

GNER

Thanks Big Al for all your support and 10 glorious years!

GNER is the official travel partner of **Alan Shearer's** testimonial

The day a hat-trick heralded a SHOOTING STAR

Alan Shearer announced his arrival on the football stage with a glorious debut hat-trick for Southampton against Arsenal at The Dell on April 9th 1988.

BOB BRUNSKELL covered the game for the Southern Daily Echo, and here Bob recalls the drama of that unforgettable day.

It was in keeping with the extraordinary player that Alan Shearer was to become that he should make a grand entrance onto the Football League stage.

A prolific youth team striker who had been tipped by his coach to become a leading player in the game, Shearer made his Southampton debut as a 17-year-old and marked the occasion with a remarkable 49-minute hat-trick in a 4-2 victory over high-flying Arsenal at The Dell.

Chris Nicholl's Saints had suffered a low-key start to 1988, failing to win a home game before the tricky encounter on April 9th with the former League leaders from North London.

Confidence was low on the pitch and in the terraces. The Hampshire club needed a tonic and Shearer, hailed by youth team coach and fellow-Geordie Dave Merrington as a natural goalscorer and an England centre-forward in the making, provided it in triple measure.

He instantly became part of Dell folklore. Not even their greatest players of old had bowed in with such a flourish. Not only did Shearer reignite Southampton's season, he condemned the Gunners to their heaviest defeat of the 1987-88 campaign.

Yet Shearer had only got into the Southampton side by chance. Danny Wallace failed a fitness test on an ankle injury and at noon, just three hours before kick-off, manager Nicholl told Shearer he would be playing. Nicholl recalls: "Alan took it in a calm, assured manner. Just as I thought he would."

Nothing fazed the man ... not even in those early, formative days. Once he got on the park he exploded, and the Gunners, without their two central defensive pillars, Tony Adams and David O'Leary, were blown apart.

Arsenal boss George Graham argued that Shearer would have found his goals harder to come by had Adams and O'Leary played and certainly their young replacements, Gus Caesar and Michael Thomas, couldn't handle Shearer and his Northern Ireland international strike partner Colin Clarke.

Nicholl countered: "George might have had two young lads playing but that should take nothing away from Alan who was young and experienced himself and just making his debut. Yet he took his chances well and Colin Clarke gave him brilliant support."

Shearer took only five minutes to score his first goal, midfielder Graham Baker provding a precise cross which the youngster, surging forward at great pace, stooped to head home from close range.

Arsenal quickly equalised courtesy of a Kevin Bond own goal, but by half-time the big guns had been emphatically silenced by a young Geordie likened by coach Merrington to the great old Bolton and England centre-forward Nat Lofthouse in style and goalscoring potency.

I'd watched Shearer playing alongside the likes of Matthew Le Tissier and Rodney Wallace for the Saints youth side and wreaking havoc in the South East Counties League.

And the dramatic story which was unfolding against Arsenal on this chilly early-spring day wasn't entirely surprising.

Shearer chased, hustled, held the line and disarmed the opposition with his instinctive ability to find good positions in and around the box. He and Clarke instantly struck up the perfect partnership. The big Irishman took the fledgling under his wing and soon had him flying high.

The two linked superbly for the second goal after 33 minutes. Shearer chased a long ball from Glenn Cockerill, won it, swept it out to Clarke, and powered on to bravely duck in among a clutch of Arsenal defenders to reach the return ball and head home.

Young Saints centre-half Mark Blake made it 3-1 just before the break, and just after it, it needed a last-ditch John Lukic save to deny Shearer his hat-trick.

But within seconds Shearer was celebrating his treble. Another cross from Clarke and a shot from Shearer which hit the underside of the bar. Before Lukic could turn and retrieve the

situation, Shearer had pounced on the rebound and dispatched it into the net.

There were still 30 minutes left but Shearer had won the game for Saints who took their foot off the gas and conceded a second goal to Arsenal late on.

Shearer, who had run himself into the ground, made way for Rod Wallace with eight minutes to go.

At 17 years and 240 days, he had become the youngster player to score a hat-trick in the old First Division, ousting the great Jimmy Greaves from the record books.

Greaves had in fact scored four for Chelsea against Portsmouth but that was halfway through his first season.

Shearer, astonishingly had done it on his debut...

The teams that famous day were:

SOUTHAMPTON Burridge, Forrest, Statham, Case, Blake, Bond, Baker, Cockerill, Clarke, Townsend, Shearer (R Wallace 82).

ARSENAL Lukic, Winterburn, Sansom, Williams, Caesar, Thomas, Rocastle, Davis, Smith, Groves (Merson 58), Hayes.

Referee: Keithe Burge (Tonypandy).

Alan through the lens

Newcastle United Club Photographer IAN HORROCKS was sitting at home one evening in July 1996 when his telephone rang. It was the start of a 10-year association with Alan Shearer that would take him around the world and give him some of his best photographs ...

IAN'S FIRST BIG ALAN SHEARER JOB WAS IN THE FAR EAST

"I was at home and out of the blue I got a phone call from Sir John Hall to tell me: pack your bags – you're going to the Far East!

"The team was going out there to play pre-season games and I had to go that next morning to Heathrow and that's where I met Alan for the first time. And the first picture I ever took of him was of him holding the Evening Chronicle front page carrying the story of his signing – I'd taken the paper down with me.

"The Chronicle had actually done a mock-up, putting Alan's head on another player's body: I'm not sure, but it might have been Rob Lee. But it looked good.

"We flew on the same plane to Singapore. Alan didn't pl in any of the games but he was part of the squad and was able to meet and get to know people.

"Kevin Keegan, the manager then, had had to get off the plane in England to get the deal finalised but he came acro later and everyone got together in the hotel.

"After arriving in Singapore, my job was to get as many pictures of him as I could. It was a bit difficult because he hadn't met the team yet and I was following him around w the camera. I did pictures of him in the gym. Some of the f pictures I did he was wearing England kit because he was awaiting the arrival of our kit-man, Ray Thompson.

"The team arrived later on and I remember walking into room where everybody was reporting for their meal. Al me them all – Kevin Keegan, Terry McDermott. Freddie Fletch and everyone.

"Al didn't play at all although he warmed up and made a appearance. We flew to Japan after the match in Singapore to Osaka. It was sweltering hot and humid.

"I got that great picture of him pouring the water over h head (left) and them all chatting.

"They had a game to play in Japan but I had to come bac The technology we have today wasn't there then and I had keep all the pictures in my bag. And then when I got back I spent all night printing them up. We did it for the local pres – it was such a big thing that they wanted everything put ou to the local papers as well."

54

ND HIS FIRST APPEARANCE WAS AT INCOLN, OF ALL PLACES

"The first game Alan played for United was a friendly at ncoln on the Friday night before the Charity Shield – and ere were people there from everywhere.

"Normally a pre-season game at Lincoln wouldn't attract uch interest but it was stowed out because Alan was aying. I didn't ask Alan to do anything special that night cause however small it is, it's still a football match.

"We stayed down in Lincoln on the Saturday and avelled on to Wembley on the Sunday for the Charity ield – and that turned into a bit of a disaster, as anchester United, who had pipped us to the league title ew months before, won 4-0."

HAT AMAZING PRESS CONFERENCE

"The Press Conference at St. James' Park was a great y. I can remember it being a warm sunny day and there ere all sorts of special things happening. The invited ests were able to come into the stadium to watch what folded in front of the world's media.

"It was like a Hollywood-type occasion – you would ve thought you were in a movie set. Outside, at the back the Leazes End stand, Alan Robson was addressing the owds on the microphone and there was me and Alan. I as able to get some fantastic exclusive shots from there, th all the fans in the car park behind him.

"There were at least 30 TV cameras, but the best sition was the one I had to myself.

"What we agreed with all the national lads was that if I t that picture they could have it.

"We needed to get Alan with his arms up wide, which is ite unusual to ask anybody to do. But it was helped by e fact that Alan was feeling so elated. That made it sier for me.

"Alan was as good as gold and the fact that we had en on the trip to the Far East together helped.

"He IS as good as gold, and very obliging. Over the ars, we've asked him to do all sorts of things, and some ings that have been suggested I wouldn't even ask him, t he will always do what he thinks is right.

"I remember doing him training for England. At the ne we had quite a few players playing for England and I ent down there – the first time I had done that.

"Alan was stretching or getting some treatment or mething and he spotted me and shouted me over and ked how I was doing, told me to come in, and all that. I ent inside a marquee and all the national press were ing crazy because they thought I was getting something ecial to myself!"

AL'S FIRST NEWCASTLE GOAL

"Alan scored his first goal for Newcastle against Wimbledon on his home debut at St. James' Park on Wednesday August 21st, 1996. It was a superb free-kick over the wall into the far corner at the Leazes End close to full-time.

"I've got a picture from the side (below) but the best picture was taken by Nigel Dobson of the Evening Chronicle. It showed him bending it around the wall.

"It's all chance, really. You take up a position but where it comes from on the pitch is pot luck, really.

"My own favourite picture comes from the game when we beat Manchester United 5-0 at St. James' in October 1996. And that's still my favourite game, too.

"The Champions League was great but to beat what was then the best team in the land by such a massive margin and in such a fabulous manner was something else.

"There was a picture of Alan and Les celebrating which summed it all up – there was a look of pure joy on both their faces.

"As a photographer you don't see how a game is going. All you are doing is concentrating on getting your next picture. My wife never understands me always wanting to watch the game again on TV.

"But you are trying to get ahead of the ball and predict where it's going to end up. So it's difficult to see how the game progresses and you don't really get the sort of perspective on it that the average fan gets.

"My favourite Alan Shearer goal came in the 7-1 defeat of Tottenham at St. James' in December '96. I got the camera on him as he came through the middle and the Spurs defenders were just bouncing off him. His strength came

through on the pictures and then he lashed the shot into the top corner of the net. You saw in that what they had brought to the club.

"Off the field, Al's a good guy – and funny as well. He's got a great sense of humour. People say he's boring and dull, but believe me he's not. He's as far from that as you can imagine."

A DIFFERENT SALUTE ...

"He's always done the regular raised-hand salute after scoring, but there was once at Blackburn when, for some reason, he did the bow-and-arrow salute ... and I didn't get it!

"Sometimes, too, you can be sat to the left, and then they run off to the right to celebrate when they score!

"Before Al's 201st goal, against Portsmouth in February, I said to him: 'I'm going to be sitting in this particular position, and if he scored would he run in my particular direction.'

"And then what did he do? In the excitement of the moment, he went off the other way! But he did run towards Serena Taylor, my club colleague photographer, who got all the close-up shots! But I did get some very good ones from where I was, showing all the fans cheering him as he ran past them celebrating.

"In summary, I've got to say that working with Alan Shearer has been a privilege and a pleasure. How many Geordies would like to be able to say they could go to work with Alan Shearer?!

"Al's been a great player, a great bloke, a great ambassador, and he's fully earned his testimonial.

"Have a fantastic night, mate – you deserve it."

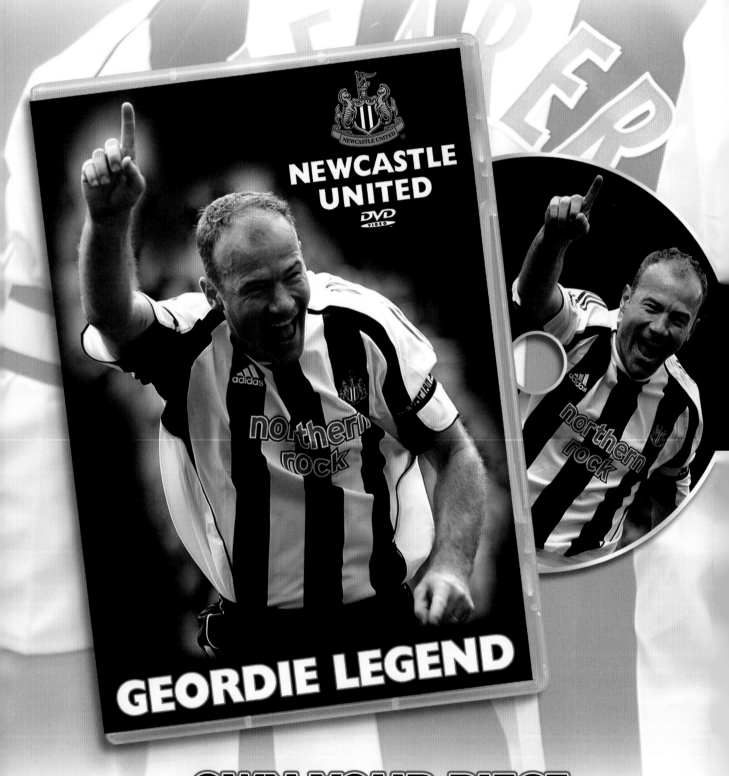

Travelling Fan Fink, our regular programme contributor, has seen **every single one** of Alan Shearer's 206 goals for United. This is his personal appreciation of what Alan has meant to him and all Newcastle supporters.

fink the fan

From Sincil Bank to the San Siro!

Not many people naa this but Big Al's forst game in a Toon shirt was for a pre-season friendly at Sincil Bank, Lincoln, in 1996.

Al scored a penalty in that game and we ran oot 2-0 winners with Philippe 'the bear' getting wor second in front of a 10,069 crowd!

After the match to celebrate his first game and goal for us, me and mee mate 'Keith The Flag' (remember the giant flag? He thought of it!) went for an Indian in the city centre and di yi naa what? It was the best Indian that we'd ever had and crazy as it soonds THIS is me owerridin' memory of that historic day!

Alan's first competitive goal then came on his home debut against Wimbledon at St. James' 12 days later from a free-kick at the Leazes End.

3-1 DOON TO 4-3 UP!

BIG AL'S BROKEN HIS HAT-TRICK DUCK!

Al's first hat-trick for the club came against Leicester City in February 1997. We were losin' 2-1 with 20 mins ti gan when Leicester added a thord to seemingly win the match. Mee mate 'Fawlty' seemed to think so anyway as he rose from his seat.

"That's it! aa've had enough!" he said as he stormed off for an orly pint of nectar! (and he wasn't the aanly one!)

Big Al then took ower and scored an amazin' hat-trick in the last 13 minutes with the winner bein' a simple tap-in from 12 inches in injury time which sent the crowd into raptures!

At the final whistle the whole team - and Al in particular - got a standin' ovation.

Aa hurried to the bar where 'Fawlty' was havin' a quiet pint. "GUESS WHAT! – SHEARER GOT A HAT-TRICK! – WE WON FOWER THREE! – WE WON FOWER THREE!" aa said to mee disbelievin' mate.

It wasn't until the gadgy sellin' the Pinks (remember them?) came roond, that he was finally convinced that aa was actually tellin' him the truth! (And the moral of this story is: NEVER leave before the end!)

FA CUP WORLD RECORDS

Al got us to two FA Cup Finals in successive seasons in the late Nineties, against Sheffield United with a 60th-minute strike in what was the aanly goal of the game in 1998, and against Spurs a year later with two extra-time goals, both played at Old Trafford. (These are the aanly occasions that aa've seen the Toon win there!)

The thing aa remember most aboot the Sheffield United trip in particular, was the fact aa had to queue for 45 mins to get served in a booza next to the groond! It was THAT packed! (A new world record!)

BEST GOAL?

So how do ye pick the best goal oot of 206? The one that sticks in everybody's mind is the 30-yard screamer against Everton at the Gallowgate End in December 2002 and of course THE record-breaker against Pompey orlier on this year aalso at the Gallowgate End.

BUT! ... the best goal as far as aa'm concerned was his penalty in his last-ever game against the mackems in wor fantastic 4-1 victory last month to score his 206th and final goal for us (a fitting end!) especially as Sunderland have a huge photo in one of their lounges of Al missin' THAT penalty against THEM six years ago! (HA! HA!)

AYE! It certainly HAS been a memorable rollercoaster ride in Big Al's ten years at the club and aa'm proud to say that aa've seen every one of his record-breakin' goals! (just!)

We'll aal miss ye, mate! - that's for certain!

HAPLESS BENNY AND THE PAN O' ONIONS!

We've had many difficult journeys on wor travels to Europe, two of them bein' wor trips in the UEFA Cup to Israel and Athens in 2004 to see Big Al and Co. play Hapoeol Bnei Sakhnin and Panionios respectively (Pronoonced: 'Pan 'o' Onions', to ye ignoramanouses's oot there!).

The game in Israel entailed a flight from Toon Airport to Dublin, then one to Rome, and then Tel Aviv via a stopower at an airbase in the Gaza Strip desert! (SIX take-offs and landings just to get there!)

On the trip to 'Pan 'o' Onions and air traffic controllers' strike was mercifully resolved in a few hours, but not in time for us to make the kick-off. We arrived at Athens airport and boarded wor coach to the groond at exactly kick-off time!

We arrived at the groond just before the start of the second half and hurried through the tornstiles!

We were telt that there was still ne score and that the forst half had been dire anyway so we hadn't missed owt! (thank god!)

The second half as it torned oot was 'dire' an' aal, but the deadlock was eventually broken three minutes from time when Big Al slotted home a penalty, sendin us into raptures! (Thanx for waitin' for us before ye scored, mate!)

Cheers Al ... and thanks for the memories!

f **FINK** (the mad-sad groundhopper!)

WATCH THE REST OF THE WORLD SHOW.

Mal life. It winks, you know. That spectacular bridge on the Quayside. Every now and again just to let me know how fabulous I'm looking. The la[ ] in the lift whispers 'first floor'. You have arrived. Bar Mal for mojitos or the Brasserie? Make mine with Mount Gay Rum. Time to dine. A comfy boo[ ] and a Cloudy Bay. Try the onion soup, it's been known to reduce Le Chef to tears. Sit back and blend into the night. A glug of Napoleon, a fine Cu[ ] later and it's all over. Morning comes. The bridge raises a disparaging eyebrow. How very co-operative and accommodating. **That's Mal lif[ ]**

Malmaison NEWCA

Hotel | Bar Mal | Brasserie | Le Petit Spa | C

He led from the front

SAYS **PAUL SCHOLES**

Manchester United star Paul Scholes played for three years with Alan Shearer for England and for more than a decade against him for the Red Devils.

And Paul says of Alan: "He was the ultimate team player – and the centre-forward no centre-half wanted to play against. He was such a handful – and his finishing was amazing."

Which is why Paul preferred to be on Alan's side rather than facing him, and he adds: "I have played against him a good few times for Manchester United and we always believed that if you could stop Alan you could stop a big portion of the opposition. But it wasn't easy stopping him!

"Playing with him was a different matter, for you knew that if you got the ball to him up front he would do something with it.

"Alan and Teddy Sheringham in particular were a great partnership for England – they were amazing playing together, and it gave us midfield players a great combination to play to.

"They seemed to have a great understanding. Teddy wasn't the quickest but Alan could feed off Teddy perfectly."

When Scholes first joined the England set-up in 1997, Alan was national team captain and the Manchester United ace adds: "He was a great captain, on and off the field.

"On the field, he led from the front, and off the field he was always there to talk to. I was a newcomer and he was already well established, but as captain he always spoke to you and made sure you were okay and made you feel welcome.

"He took being captain very seriously."

Scholes, however, has done one thing that Alan never has –and that is scored a hat-trick in a Newcastle-Manchester United game!

He did it when the Red Devils won 6-2 at St. James' in 2002-03, and he says of it: "That was one of my peak games for Manchester United."

It came a season after a dramatic seven-goal St. James' Park thriller went Newcastle's way, 4-3.

Alan's shot brought the winner after Manchester United had clawed their way back from 3-1 down to 3-3, but it went in off Wes Brown and was later credited to the Manchester United defender as an own goal.

Alan has always said the goal should have been his, but Scholes says cheekily: "It was well off target before it hit Wes and went in – but I don't think Alan will miss that one too badly, with all the goals he's got to his name!"

And he added: "I'd like to wish one of this country's finest-ever players all the best for his testimonial. Alan has had a great career and deserves this special night."

Alan was Rooney hero

[W]AYNE ROONEY was two-[an]d-a-half years old when [Al]an Shearer made his [fo]otball League debut in [Ap]ril 1988. He has grown up [ad]miring Shearer ... and now [th]ey have shared the same [Pr]emier League stage.

Alan believes Wayne is [de]stined for the very top of the [fo]otball tree, and has said so [m]ore than once.

And Wayne, now 20, told us [ex]clusively what Alan Shearer [h]as meant to him in his [yo]ung years.

"I am constantly asked who [m]y heroes were growing up - [an]d it is always the same [an]swer. Duncan Ferguson, [be]cause I was an Everton fan [an]d all Everton fans love Big [Du]nc, and Alan Shearer because [h]e was England's Number Nine [an]d that was what I dreamed of [be]ing one day.

"Both of them figured strongly [in] my desire and determination [to] be a professional footballer, [bu]t none moreso than Alan [Sh]earer, England's centre-[for]ward.

"My early memories of Al [we]re during Euro 96 when I was [1]0. The whole country had gone [foo]tball mad - I didn't have to as [I w]as already – and England [we]re outstanding during the [to]urnament and none were [be]tter than Shearer.

"Me, my mates and families watched all the matches together, especially the England games when the atmosphere was fantastic.

"I particularly remember the match against Holland when England destroyed them and Super Al scored a great goal smashed in his customary style into the top of the net.

"I went out and practised Al's technique until it went too dark to see the goalposts!

"I have been privileged like all of us here tonight to watch some fantastic performances from him for both club and country, and I have also been privileged to be on the same pitch as him.

Unfortunately, I have never been lucky enough to be in the same team as him, but I am pretty sure we would have blended well together.

"Alan talked a few weeks ago about how he had been blessed and lived his dream. Alan, I would personally like to thank you for helping make my dream come true, for watching you made me realise all I ever wanted to do was to be a professional footballer

"I hope it's a great night, Alan, and all the best to you and your family for the future."

TRIBUTES FROM OLD TRAFFORD

ALAN IS THE PROFESSIONAL'S PROFESSIONAL

Manchester United manager Sir Alex Ferguson has described Alan Shearer as "the professional's professional".

Speaking at the HMV Lifetime Achievement Award dinner in London last month, Sir Alex said he did not hold any grudge over Alan's decision to join the other United – Newcastle – in July 1996.

He said: "There are no hard feelings that he turned down Manchester United. Football is football. I'm sorry he didn't join us, but there you are."

And Sir Alex added: "Alan is the professional's professional.

"The great thing about Alan is that he's had some serious injuries. It takes a lot of determination and will to get back from serious injuries but he has done it a number of times.

"That's the hallmark of someone who has great courage. Some players cannot do that, but Alan has."

He added: "Alan's a centre-forward. In an era when the game is changing in terms of terminology of what a player is, he is a centre-forward.

"He is a natural centre-forward in the tradition of the British game. It's not easy for the lad because as the changes of game have come along the roles of players have changed, but he has never changed as a centre-forward.

"The memory of Alan is his percentage of shots on target. If there was an opportunity to have a strike at goal he would get it on target. That was a great asset he had and it stood him apart from other centre-forwards."

He gave us all a great variety of goals.

We give you a great variety of music.

A place in history

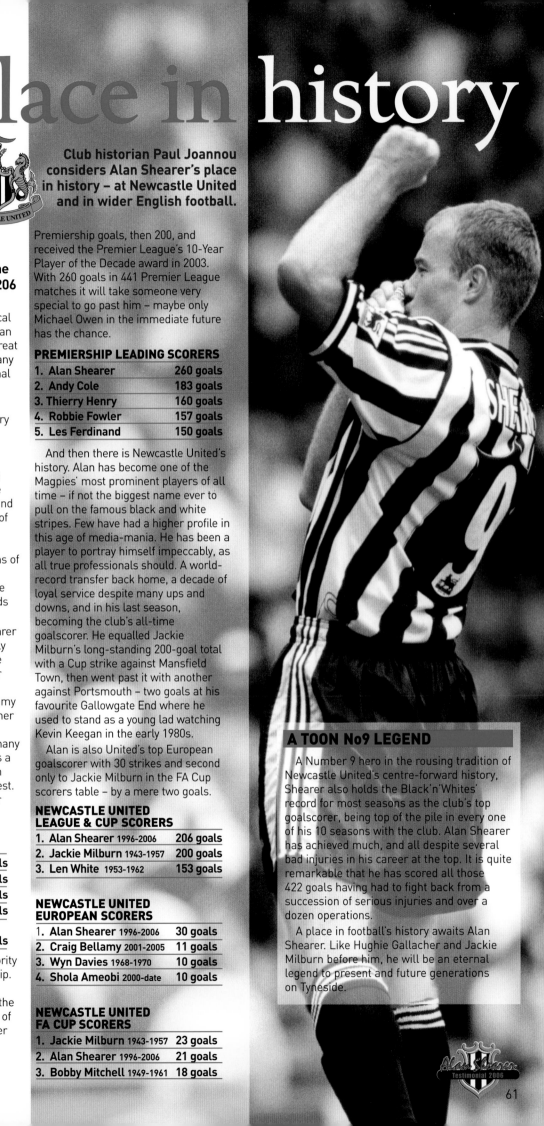

Club historian Paul Joannou considers Alan Shearer's place in history – at Newcastle United and in wider English football.

ALAN SHEARER holds a very special place in Newcastle United's history at the top of the all-time goalscorers list with 206 first-class goals to his name.

Yet Alan not only has a place in local folklore here in the North-East, he can also be set alongside all the other great strikers in English football – and in any era since football became the national sport over a century ago.

Only a handful of English strikers good enough to have reached the very top in international football have totalled over 400 first-class goals in their career. Alan Shearer with an aggregate of 422 joins that very elite bunch of strikers which includes the likes of Dixie Dean, Steve Bloomer and Jimmy Greaves. Many of the greats of the past didn't get to that 400-goal milestone. Nat Lofthouse didn't. Nor did Tommy Lawton. And in terms of out-and-out centre-forwards in the traditional mould only the great Dixie Dean from the inter-war years stands alongside Shearer.

In international football Alan Shearer ranks with the very best as well. Only four other players have scored more goals for England than Alan's 30. Sir Bobby Charlton tops the list with 49 goals, followed by Gary Lineker, Jimmy Greaves and his Newcastle and former England team-mate Michael Owen, who – before the World Cup in Germany – is on 35 goals. Owen of course has a terrific opportunity to take over from Charlton as his country's all-time best. And no-one from Scotland, Wales or Northern Ireland has scored more goals than Tyneside's favourite son.

ENGLAND LEADING SCORERS

. Bobby Charlton	49 goals	
. Gary Lineker	48 goals	
. Jimmy Greaves	44 goals	
. Michael Owen	35 goals	
. Alan Shearer, Nat Lofhouse, Tom Finney	30 goals	

Alan Shearer has played the majority of his club football in the Premiership. And since its introduction back in 1992-93, Alan is way out in front as the competition's top goal-getter ahead of Andy Cole, Les Ferdinand – two other United No. 9s of course – Robbie Fowler and Teddy Sheringham. He was the first player to score 100

Premiership goals, then 200, and received the Premier League's 10-Year Player of the Decade award in 2003. With 260 goals in 441 Premier League matches it will take someone very special to go past him – maybe only Michael Owen in the immediate future has the chance.

PREMIERSHIP LEADING SCORERS

1. Alan Shearer	260 goals
2. Andy Cole	183 goals
3. Thierry Henry	160 goals
4. Robbie Fowler	157 goals
5. Les Ferdinand	150 goals

And then there is Newcastle United's history. Alan has become one of the Magpies' most prominent players of all time – if not the biggest name ever to pull on the famous black and white stripes. Few have had a higher profile in this age of media-mania. He has been a player to portray himself impeccably, as all true professionals should. A world-record transfer back home, a decade of loyal service despite many ups and downs, and in his last season, becoming the club's all-time goalscorer. He equalled Jackie Milburn's long-standing 200-goal total with a Cup strike against Mansfield Town, then went past it with another against Portsmouth – two goals at his favourite Gallowgate End where he used to stand as a young lad watching Kevin Keegan in the early 1980s.

Alan is also United's top European goalscorer with 30 strikes and second only to Jackie Milburn in the FA Cup scorers table – by a mere two goals.

NEWCASTLE UNITED LEAGUE & CUP SCORERS

1. Alan Shearer	1996-2006	206 goals
2. Jackie Milburn	1943-1957	200 goals
3. Len White	1953-1962	153 goals

NEWCASTLE UNITED EUROPEAN SCORERS

1. Alan Shearer	1996-2006	30 goals
2. Craig Bellamy	2001-2005	11 goals
3. Wyn Davies	1968-1970	10 goals
4. Shola Ameobi	2000-date	10 goals

NEWCASTLE UNITED FA CUP SCORERS

1. Jackie Milburn	1943-1957	23 goals
2. Alan Shearer	1996-2006	21 goals
3. Bobby Mitchell	1949-1961	18 goals

A TOON No9 LEGEND

A Number 9 hero in the rousing tradition of Newcastle United's centre-forward history, Shearer also holds the Black'n'Whites' record for most seasons as the club's top goalscorer, being top of the pile in every one of his 10 seasons with the club. Alan Shearer has achieved much, and all despite several bad injuries in his career at the top. It is quite remarkable that he has scored all those 422 goals having had to fight back from a succession of serious injuries and over a dozen operations.

A place in football's history awaits Alan Shearer. Like Hughie Gallacher and Jackie Milburn before him, he will be an eternal legend to present and future generations on Tyneside.

Al ruined my 18th birthday...
but I forgive him!

The first thing that I remember about Alan Shearer is him ruining my 18th birthday.

Newcastle were at home to Blackburn that day, I was having a party on the night and as usual there were a load of us standing in The Scoreboard.

Andy Cole had put us 1-0 up, then Shearer came off the bench on his comeback from injury, and within about five minutes he'd popped in the equaliser at the Gallowgate and ran past all of us lot with his arm in the air celebrating.

Cheers Alan, thanks very much!

He's made up for it since then though, so I'll forgive him now.

I could talk all day about the goals which stand out. I remember the first one against Wimbledon, the game against Leicester when he scored a hat-trick to help us win 4-3 after being 3-1 down, there was that volley against Schmeichel when he was in goal for Villa, and of course the volley against Everton. And who could forget the 5-0 against Manchester United, when he scored that day?

It's funny how things stick in your mind, but I also remember a goal against Blackburn at Ewood Park. I think he scored twice that night actually, when he changed his celebration and did this daft little routine to do a pose like he was holding a bow and arrow or something.

It was pretty bad, but I think he must have realised that when he saw it on the telly and the next goal it was the boring old arm-up-in-the-air routine again!

Off the pitch, Alan is very dry, he has a great sense of humour and he hammers me and Ant every time he sees us.

But we give as good as we get, and we often text him when we see him sitting on Match of the Day wearing a tie that doesn't match his shirt, or a pair of shoes that don't go with his suit.

Hopefully, when he retires, he'll have more time to sort his dress sense out.

He might even decide to come in the jungle with us actually, now he'll have a bit spare time on his hands.

The thing is, he'd probably end up winning it. He'd eat more bugs than anyone else, he'd do the challenges twice as quick as the rest of the competitors, and would probably end up winning the thing.

He's sickening like that.

But seriously, Alan Shearer has put Newcastle on the map – both the team and the city.

Wherever we go in the world, as soon as we say where we are from, and who we support, Alan Shearer is mentioned whether we are in Tokyo, the Philippines, Australia - anywhere in the world.

Whatever he chooses to do when he finishes playing, he will be a success. He's been a success in everything else he's done, so why should that change once he hangs up his boots?

Alan Shearer is one in a million, and I wish him all the best tonight and in the future.

DEC

ANT AND DEC

We've got some Witchity grubs ready for Al!

I remember that game that Dec mentioned, on his 18th birthday when Shearer wrecked it.

But I also remember thinking at that time that Alan would probably end up abroad if he left Blackburn. I'd never have dreamt that we would sign him.

I always felt he'd move to a club like Juventus or Barcelona, but thankfully for us he decided to come home.

He may not have won the trophies, but he's certainly given us plenty of moments to remember over the years.

We were away in Japan when we heard the news that Kevin Keegan had broken the world record to sign him.

It was unbelievable. Here we were on the other side of the world, and the only place we wanted to be was standing outside the back of the Leazes End with thousands of other Geordies welcoming him home.

The impact he has had on the club is amazing, there must be no better feeling for him to score at St. James' Park and have the whole stadium singing his name.

When people talk to us about Alan, there is an impression that he comes across as very sensible in interviews and

Congratulations, Alan – you'll always be the Local Hero! MARK KNOPFLER

things like that, but when you get to know him he is as down-to-earth as the come.

We see a lot of stars in our line of wo but I can honestly say that the only tim was starstruck was when I met Alan Shearer.

But he makes you feel at ease with hi and he takes the mick like you wouldn believe. Alan has a great sense of humo and he gives as good as he gets – with a little bit more for good measure.

For some reason, he hammers me about my height, and says I've got a big forehead. If you look closely, his forehe is getting bigger as well the rate his hai receding, but we won't go into that!

I don't know what Alan will choose do once he finally hangs up his boots. Obviously TV punditry is high on his l of options, but I think he is cut out for career in management.

If he can be as successful a manager he has been a player, then we'll all be happy – especially if it's here at St. James' Park.

In the meantime, we'll have to wait see what he chooses to do, but if he fancies coming to the jungle with us t we'd be happy to have him there. Alan Shearer eating witchity grubs has a certain ring to it, doesn't it?

It goes without saying that I wish hi all the best for his testimonial game t evening, and I have no doubts we will seeing a lot of more of Alan Shearer ir years to come.

AN

JIMMY NAIL SAYS: I was all set to travel north and sit through the great man's last competitive match, against the mighty Chelsea at St. James' Park. A fitting time, place and opponent for the Premier League's undisputed goal-king to take one final bow, the maestro in communion with his adoring fans. And what happens? He's ambushed by the Mackems! That one we'll not forget.

Can it really be true? Will we never again watch that famous finger shoot skywards as its owner peels away from the opposition's penalty area, grin wide, job done? Like most big deals, it hasn't fully sunk in yet. All things must pass, said a Beatle. Sooner or later the curtain must fall. So here we are. Big Al's had a great run, he's all done and it's golf and a bit of gardening. Aye, that'll be right.

Will he help us, in a managerial capacity, get our hands on some silverware? You wouldn't bet against it. Only a fan can understand that empty hollow feeling, and Alan's a fan. He's just like all the rest of us in that respect. I'm grateful to him for the choices he made, for what he's done while wearing the black and white shirt, and for what he's given, to football in general and Tyneside in particular.

My favourite Shearer goal? The one he put past Peter Schmeichel, in goal for Aston Villa, a sensational diagonal side-footed volley which flew right across the 6-yard box, coming to rest in the top corner. That goal had absolutely everything.

PRIME MINISTER TONY BLAIR SAYS:
Only the very best footballers can dominate the game at the highest level. It takes talent, presence, bravery and dedication. Alan Shearer has all these qualities in abundance. You can't score 30 goals in three consecutive Premiership seasons, lead England agonisingly close to a Euro-final, or become Newcastle's record goalscorer without them.

And for Newcastle fans, Alan Shearer is also special because his love and commitment for this club are as intense as their own. He grew up here and supported this club as a child. But he also chose to come home when he could have gone anywhere in the world. This created a special bond with the fans here which grew stronger every time that familiar raised-arm salute was seen.

But the measure of the man is more than his goals. Alan Shearer has come back from injuries that would have finished lesser men and adapted his game accordingly. This took courage and intelligence. Allied to his natural talent and mental resolution, it made him arguably – although there won't be much argument at St. James' Park – the best English player of his generation.

I am pleased to pay tribute for all he has done for Newcastle and English football and wish him every success for the future. He deserves it.

ROBSON GREEN SAYS: "I wasn't there when Shearer broke the record. I was filming on the roof of a tower block three miles away that fortunately overlooked St. James' Park.

During a long scene in the afternoon we had to stop filming. What stopped the sequence was a sound, a sound from the stadium, a roar so loud and unmistakably beautiful that it could mean only one thing. I and nearly a hundred others fixed our gaze towards the stadium. 'He's done it!' I shouted 'He's broken the record'. Ninety-nine faces, 20 percent of which were from different parts of the world posed the question 'who's broken the record?' 'Alan Shearer' came my reply. 'How do you know, Robson?' My answer was simple but it was the only answer a passionate Newcastle fan would understand … 'I just know'.

When Shearer's name is mentioned, whether you are on top of a roof three miles from St. James's Park or in a restaurant situated under a rain forest in Malaysia, everyone knows who you are talking about. That is why there is only one Alan Shearer.

Since the age of seven I like you have applauded and sung the names of players who have graced the turf of St. James'. When it comes to singing the name of Alan Shearer it is sung out of loyalty. But more importantly out of love. That is what makes Shearer unique. Newcastle fans not only admire and respect him … we love him.

He has given us memories and moments of genius that will stay in our minds forever. But tonight we will, with a heavy heart, be forced to acknowledge that his gesture, his salute, will not be the celebration of a goal, but a goodbye wave to all of us who love him.

'Keep The Legend Alive'

Commemorating his glorious career, a prestigious limited edition Coalport figurine in association with Alan Shearer and Newcastle United Football Club.

Strictly a limited edition of just 5,000 sold on a first come first served basis, so early ordering is recommended to avoid disappointment.

- Made by Coalport, the renowned English bone china company - one of the world's leading manufacturers of fine figurines

- Designed and sculpted by one of the most highly regarded artists in the ceramics industry

- Each piece individually numbered, with a specimen signature

- Certificate of Authenticity

- Not available in any other retail outlet

- Approved by NUFC

- Incredible value at £199

'I am very impressed by the professional way the figure has been made'

COALPORT®
EST. 1750

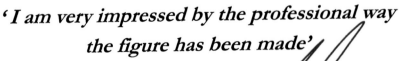

Available from the Official Club Store at St. James' Park

NEWCAST
UNITED

THE NSPCC AND ITS WORK

**Alan Shearer has supported the NSPCC for many years.
He appeared in the award-winning national TV adverts that launched the
FULL STOP campaign a few years ago and is also an active fundraiser.
We would like to thank Alan for all his support and we are extremely
grateful to be one of the beneficiaries of his testimonial.**

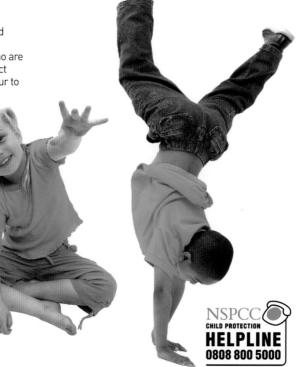

Here in the North-East the NSPCC runs four fantastic projects for children and
young people.

In Newcastle, at Brighton Grove, we offer a therapeutic service for children who are
'looked after' and have been abused. This involves the use of family therapy, direct
and indirect play therapy and counselling. The team works with children aged four to
18 and also supports their carers.

In Sunderland our Kaleidoscope project works with children and
young people who display sexually harmful behaviour. The aim is to try
and understand and change their behaviour and to support their
families. The team carries out one-to-one work as well as family and
group work.

The North East Specialist Investigation Service, based in Jesmond,
is one of a network of independent teams. They work in partnership
with police, social services and other statutory child care agencies,
primarily to investigate organised, institutional and professional
abuse.

Our schools team based in Blyth works in a number of schools in
Northumberland offering one-to-one consultations and group work.

As well as our local projects, children in the North-East can access
the NSPCC in a variety of ways. One such way is through
There4me.com, a unique interactive website designed to help
young people aged 12 to 16 years by giving easily accessible
information, advice and support on the issues important to them

The NSPCC Child Protection Helpline is another vital service helping
keep children safe in the North-East. The Helpline provides free advice,
counselling and information to anyone who thinks that a child may be at risk.
In 2005, the Helpline received 1,682 calls from Newcastle upon Tyne alone.

SAMARITAN'S PURSE

Samaritan's Purse is a non-profit,
Christian organisation. We aim to
provide love, hope, development and
immediate relief for needy
communities in the grip of poverty
or following a war, natural disaster,
disease or famine, whilst
demonstrating God's compassion in
action.

Operation Christmas Child is our largest
programme and in 2005 we increased the
number of gift-filled shoe boxes collected in
the UK to 1.18 million. This means that more
than a million children in 13 impoverished
countries received what might have been
their first-ever Christmas gift.

Samaritan's Purse also runs programmes
and teams aimed at developing children. For
example, soccer teams will be going to
Russia and Liberia in the summer. Trained
soccer coaches and proven quality amateur
footballers use their skills and energy to
offer fun coaching sessions to needy
children.

An emergency usually comes "out of the
blue". It is unexpected and devastating in its
impact. Samaritan's Purse is involved in
these situations. We aim to match resources

to needs, personnel to situations,
capabilities to opportunities. For example,
our response to the earthquake in Pakistan
consisted of providing personnel, emergency
household items and longer-term
programmes.

Our long-term development programmes
are mainly aimed at fighting HIV and AIDS
and providing communities with safe
drinking water.

One of Samaritan's Purse's "Safe Water
for Life" projects is a borehole rehabilitation
programme in Mozambique. The
Chicualacuala district has been severely
affected by five years of severe drought and
a lack of access to water. Thirty-five percent
of boreholes in the district are non-
operational. The remaining functional
boreholes are overused by communities and
currently serve a population of 39,884
people. Samaritan's Purse is setting up
borehole maintenance teams and an
estimated 15,340 beneficiaries will benefit
from improved boreholes.

**Samaritan's Purse and particularly the
staff and volunteers at the Newcastle
Warehouse would like to thank Alan Shearer
for including us on his
list of charities!**

Samaritan's Purse
INTERNATIONAL RELIEF

"Alan has always been a Nº1 goalscorer"

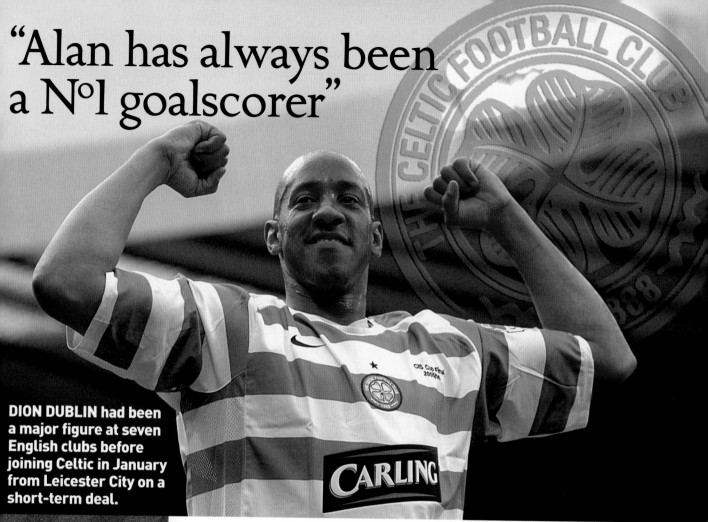

DION DUBLIN had been a major figure at seven English clubs before joining Celtic in January from Leicester City on a short-term deal.

Thirty-seven last month, Dublin is one of the few players left in the British game who can claim seniority over Alan Shearer!

He joined Norwich City from non-league Oakham United in March 1988 – a month before Alan made his Southampton debut.

Their careers have run parallel in terms of timespan, but in terms of achievement Dion readily admits he is not in the same league as the man who captained England and Newcastle United and in whose honour tonight's match with Celtic is being played.

"Alan Shearer has been the best-performing British player we have had in many, many years," Dion says emphatically. "And I think that is a sentiment echoed by 99 percent of players in this country. It is an honour to be part of his testimonial tonight.

"He has always been a Number One goalscorer for the whole of my career.

"Over the years, you've always known that the name of Alan Shearer has been going to appear in the list of top goalscorers in the country.

"You always hear the `Shearer, Shearer, Shearer' chant and there's not a lot you can teach him when it comes to scoring goals."

Alan was England captain when Dion was called into the national squad four times in 1998 and 1999, and the Leicester-born veteran remembers how Alan welcomed him into the group and made him feel comfortable and relaxed.

He says: "I was a 28-year-old newcomer to the England set-up for a short spell but merely being around Alan you could see the respect he commanded. He made me really welcome and relaxed me completely.

"Off the pitch, he was a leader, and on the pitch he was a captain – even if he didn't have the armband.

"He has always been a shining example of how to be a centre-forward, and in future years coaches will show videos and DVDs of him as an instruction course for up-and-coming youngsters.

"I love playing against players like Alan Shearer – hard but fair, he whacks you and you whack him and he never grumbles or complains, which is just the way I like it too.

"Mind you, perhaps it's a good job he's not playing against us tonight because he might have given me one final good whacking!"

Three years ago, on the eve of his 34th birthday and by now converted from centre-forward to centre-half, Dion travelled to St. James' with Aston Villa.

Sent on as a substitute with Villa 1-0 behind to a first-half Nobby Solano goal, Dion headed a 69th-minute equaliser ... but he went away from St. James' with more than a point.

"Because that day I swapped shirts with Alan Shearer and among my collection that's up at the top," he says. "It's a great honour to have swapped shirts with a legend.

"I remember that goal because Alan was meant to be marking me for a change, but I outpaced him in the Zimmer Frame Stakes and headed it in!

"I have played against Alan a couple of times and he's pretty elusive – and there's always that added factor that he's going to have a go at goal from any angle and at any time.

"I wouldn't for a moment put myself in Alan's class, because I'm nowhere near, but, like Alan, I like to play in high-pressure games because it gets the best out of you. And Alan has always been like that – a big-game player who produces his best in the high-pressure games."

Meanwhile, the Celtic fans, who flooded into Newcastle for Peter Beardsley's testimonial in 1999, will be here in force again tonight to back their own side as well as pay tribute to a player for whom there is a very healthy respect north of the border.

Says Dion: "The fans up here do respect Alan and what he has achieved and they are really taking this one as a big game. There's been a real buzz about Alan's testimonial, with all the Celtic fans organising buses to Tyneside, as well as Roy Keane's testimonial earlier this week.

"I'm enjoying playing for Celtic – Rob Kelly at Leicester agreed to let me come up here for the rest of the season and I've already added a Cup medal to my collection although whether I got a Championship medal depended on whether I played enough games this season.

"I'm really looking forward to playing in Alan's testimonial, and looking forward to seeing him again. We're not close buddies as such, but whenever we meet we always have a little chat and I'm honoured to be part of tonight.

"And there's one other reason I'm looking forward to seeing Alan tonight – he still owes me twenty quid!"

THE BHOYS ARE BACK IN TOON

THE BHOYS ARE BACK IN TOON

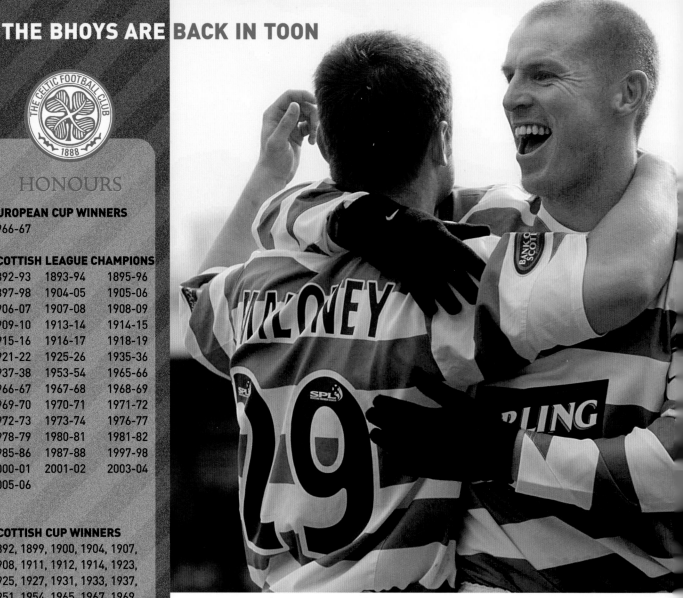

HONOURS

EUROPEAN CUP WINNERS
1966-67

SCOTTISH LEAGUE CHAMPIONS

1892-93	1893-94	1895-96
1897-98	1904-05	1905-06
1906-07	1907-08	1908-09
1909-10	1913-14	1914-15
1915-16	1916-17	1918-19
1921-22	1925-26	1935-36
1937-38	1953-54	1965-66
1966-67	1967-68	1968-69
1969-70	1970-71	1971-72
1972-73	1973-74	1976-77
1978-79	1980-81	1981-82
1985-86	1987-88	1997-98
2000-01	2001-02	2003-04
2005-06		

SCOTTISH CUP WINNERS

1892, 1899, 1900, 1904, 1907,
1908, 1911, 1912, 1914, 1923,
1925, 1927, 1931, 1933, 1937,
1951, 1954, 1965, 1967, 1969,
1971, 1972, 1974, 1975, 1977,
1980, 1985, 1988, 1989, 1995,
2001, 2004, 2005

LEAGUE CUP WINNERS

1956-57	1957-58	1965-66
1966-67	1967-68	1968-69
1969-70	1974-75	1982-83
1997-98	1999-2000	2000-01
2005-06		

WELCOME TO OUR VISITORS

ARTUR BORUC GOALKEEPER
Polish international keeper who arrived on a season-long loan deal from Legia Warsaw in the summer of 2005. Strong and commanding, Boruc has cemented his first-team place with a string of top-class performances.
Born: Siedlce, Poland, 20.2.80

DIANBOB BALDE
DEFENDER
Fans' favourite who joined on a free transfer from French club Toulouse in the summer of 2001. A Guinean international, he proved Celtic's most improved player in 2002-03 and the Celtic fans voted him Player of the Year.
Born: Marseille, France, 5.10.75

PAUL TELFER DEFENDER
Celtic manager Gordon Strachan had the experienced Telfer at Southampton and Coventry. He was recruited by Celtic last summer and quickly established himself as a first-team regular.
Born: Edinburgh, 21.10.71

STANISLAV VARGA DEFENDER
Slovakian international who signed for Celtic in July 2003 from Sunderland on a free transfer. Composed and commanding, he has forged a first-class defensive partnership with Bobo Balde.
Born: Lipany, Slovakia, 8.10.72

ROY KEANE
MIDFIELDER
Former Manchester United and 65-times-capped Republic of Ireland captain, Keane was taken to Parkhead by Gordon Strachan last December, thus fulfilling a lifetime's ambition to play for Celtic.
Born: Cork, Republic of Ireland, 10.8.71

Celtic FOOTBALL CLUB

NEIL LENNON MIDFIELDER
A £6m signing from Leicester City in 2000, the determined, influential and hard-working Northern Ireland international has become a hero of the Celtic fans with a long run of top-notch displays.
Born: Lurgan, Northern Ireland, 25.6.71

STILIAN PETROV
MIDFIELDER
Bulgarian star who came through a difficult start at Celtic after signing from CSKA Sofia and blossomed under Martin O'Neill. A fast, skilful box-to-box player, he is one of Britain's finest midfield operators.
Born: Bulgaria, 5.7.79

ALAN THOMPSON MIDFIELDER
Ex-United Geordie who also played for Bolton and Aston Villa before joining Celtic for £2.75m in September 2001. His sweet left foot is a deadly weapon at set-pieces and he was picked for Sven-Goran Eriksson's England squad for the 2003-04 friendly against Sweden.
Born: Newcastle, 22.12.73

SHUNSUKE NAKAMURA MIDFIELDER
Japanese international midfield star with over 50 caps, signed from Reggina in July last year. A player of exceptional flair and vision, he hopes to further his reputation in the forthcoming World Cup.
Born: Kanagawa, Japan, 24.6.78

DION DUBLIN STRIKER/DEFENDER
Veteran striker who commanded a £5.75m fee when he moved from Coventry City to Aston Villa in November 1998, having four years earlier won the Premiership title with Manchester United. Dion moved from Leicester to Celtic midway through the 2005-06 season and played a part in Celtic's Championship success.
Born: Leicester 22.4.69

JOHN HARTSON STRIKER
Martin O'Neill paid £6m to sign the bustling Welsh international forward in 2001 and steadily established himself as a vital member of the squad. A back injury kept him out of the 2003 UEFA Cup Final but he has maintained high standards.
Born: Swansea, 5.4.75

SHUAN MALONEY
STRIKER
Diminutive Malaysian-born Maloney has recovered from a serious knee injury to make himself a regular fixture in Gordon Strachan's team. Exciting and inventive, he is a genuine crowd-pleaser.
Born: Mirri, Malaysia, 24.1.83

AIDEN McGEADY STRIKER
The most talked-about youngster in Scottish football, who has chosen to represent Ireland rather than his native Scotland, burst on the scene in dramatic style and operates at his best in the role behind the strikers.
Born: Glasgow, 4.4.86

MACIEJ ZURAWSKI STRIKER
An explosive goalscorer, the Polish international signed for Celtic from Wisla Krakow of Poland last July. Quick-footed, strong and aggressive, he is a major talent in the international game.
Born: Poznan, 12.9.76

SHUNSUKE NAKAMURA

JOHN HARTSON

THE MANAGER

GORDON STRACHAN
Edinburgh-born Strachan started out with Dundee in 1974 but achieved fame with Aberdeen where, under Alex Ferguson's management, the Dons won the European Cup-winners' Cup. Ron Atkinson paid £500,000 to take the little midfielder to Old Trafford in 1984 and after five years with Manchester United he moved to Leeds United where, under Howard Wilkinson, Strachan was a central cog in the exciting side that took the 1992 Championship.

The winner of 50 Scotland caps, Strachan was voted the PFA Player of the Year in 1990-91 at Leeds, and after moving to Coventry City in 1995 established a Premiership record by playing at the age of 40.

He then became manager of the Highfield Road club but was sacked after relegation in 2001.

Within weeks Strachan was appointed manager of Southampton, but in March 2004 he announced his resignation in order to be able to spend more time with his family and take a break from the game.

That break lasted only until June 2005, when he succeeded Martin O'Neill as manager of Celtic, and he steered the Celts to this year's Scottish Championship with six games to spare.

That achievement brought him the latest Scottish Manager of the Year accolade.

SMC
Systems Integration

Sign here please Alan!

...wcastle United's Retail Administrator ...ire Moran looks after the fan mail ...ch pours into St. James' Park on a ...y basis. She tells Ian Willis how she ...nages to cope with such a huge ...ume of mail - on top of her ...-time job!

...basically deal with everything that comes ...St. James' Park for Alan, and that ...unts to at least a couple of hundred items ...week," says Claire.

...here are certain times when Alan gets ...e mail, such as when he announced he ...going to retire at the end of last season. ...k people saw it as a last chance to get ...s signed by Alan, so we were bombarded ...material!

...nd when Alan scored his 201st goal to ...k the record against Portsmouth, in the ...k that followed we were inundated with ...ratulations cards and letters.

...n an average week, I divide his mail up ...three sections. The first section is made ...f things people want signed, like shirts, ...ographs, posters and match ...rammes.

...he second section of his mail is the ...rs, most of them wishing him well or as I ...offering congratulations if he has scored ...al or had a particularly good game.

...he final section deals with requests for ...to help out with charities, or make a

personal appearance at a school or an event. All this is passed on to his agents, and they deal with it from there.

"But every single piece of mail that comes in is dealt with, and we keep a huge database of all the requests that come in for Alan.

"Alan has a signing session four or five times a season, where he will keep an afternoon free and come up to St. James' to work his way through the pile of items. We can oblige with most of the requests that come in, where Alan will sign something for a fan and I will have it posted back.

"There are some requests every once in a while where we can't help – I remember one fan wrote to us asking if he could have the bandage he wore when he split his head open in 2002!

"The mail comes in from all over the world. We get stuff from Australia, all over the Far East, as well as items from places across Europe.

"Some of the things that come in from the likes of Japan and Hong Kong have the local good luck messages, things like the Chinese

writing and keepsakes. Some of the things that come in are really interesting, and I make sure Alan gets to see it all.

"Some items have arrived in an envelope with 'Alan Shearer, Newcastle' as the address, but it still finds its way to him!

"It's quite a time-consuming thing to do, but I really enjoy it and it is a pleasure for me to take it on. I've done the job for the last five seasons, and I'm sure the fan mail will keep on coming in to the club when Alan retires.

"Alan enjoys seeing the things that come in for him as well. I'd imagine as a footballer you must be doing something right if you get hundreds of bits of post each week.

"I know he's grateful that I deal with the post for him.

"When I got married earlier in the season, he sent us a card and a present and also sent one of his match shirts to the reception for my husband, Michael.

"That was a nice touch from Alan, though I wasn't too happy when Michael said that it made his day!"